D0534329

THE Making It GUIDE TO CRAFTING

THE Making It

GUIDE TO CRAFTING

 BY THE CREATORS OF Making It

Foreword by **NICK OFFERMAN**

Introduction by **DAYNA ISOM JOHNSON**

Written by Liz Welker

Photography by Nicole Hill Gerulat

ABRAMS, NEW YORK

TABLE OF CONTENTS

A CRAFTER'S PANTRY

FASTER CRAFTS

MASTER CRAFTS

FOREWORD

BY NICK OFFERMAN

"Hey, you wanna do some crafts?"

What image or feeling does this question conjure for you? Something frivolous, like a "hobby"? Tracing your surprisingly turkey-like hand onto a paper plate? Or something more substantial, like a "discipline"? Soaking lengths of cane with which to weave a seat, perhaps. Do you roll your eyes, or do you feel the thrill of impending creativity?

I think that the term "crafting" for many people brings to mind activities in which your kindergarten teacher or your grandmother might have involved you once upon a time—keeping you occupied with scissors, glue, and crayons so you wouldn't get into any mischief out behind the gymnasium. I certainly may have given this question an eye-roll at certain points in my life, when I had more pressing matters at hand, like getting back to an imperative video game, or napping.

However, in hindsight, it's plain to me that my onetime ambivalence to crafting was just a symptom of a larger devotion to escapism in my young life. Before I discovered that I could, and indeed would, make my living entirely by crafting (making wooden items for sale, building theater scenery, writing books and songs, and, I guess most substantially, fabricating performances as an entertainer), I would, on occasion, succumb to the human condition in which one effectually says, "Ah, why try? I'm not good at it."

In this age of luxury and readily available comforts for purchase, it grows ever easier to throw up one's hands and give in to personal apathy and mediocrity. People often say to me, "I've tried knitting and I sucked at it." or "I can't make anything. I'm hopeless." I always gently disagree with them and then cite my own clumsy history in my woodworking shop. I have made some very beautiful pieces of furniture, sure, as well as some canoes and ukuleles in my life, but boy howdy, did I have to first make mistake after mistake for years and years, ruining a lot of good lumber (or at least rendering it into smaller pieces of good lumber). Nothing that we can create masterfully ever comes easy, just like playing piano or guitar—it takes practice.

On top of that notion, I also remind people that there are virtually no limits to the kinds of things we can craft. You had trouble knitting? Try hand sewing! No dice? Okay, try embroidery! You are opposed to cloth in general? Perhaps you're a nudist? All right, how about blacksmithing? Hang on—on second thought, you're going to definitely want to wear at least an apron for that. But if I limit my definition of crafting to simply "assembling/shaping some combination of materials into a new creation for practical use or aesthetic pleasure," then the crafting world is truly your oyster. All you have to do is make a start.

I have a good friend named Pat Riot who is a very talented visual artist, but he hates conventional tools and materials. So, in a nonconforming (bratty) way, he makes his artworks with whatever stuff he happens to find, and the results are even more impressive, because he didn't just paint a "boring, old" painting. For example, he has a very popular series of large pointillism portraits of baseball players, like 3' x 4', done entirely in tiny chewed bits of chewing gum. For the different colors he requires, he just uses different flavors. He relates the gum thematically to the chewing gum that used to come in packages of baseball cards, but all I know is that these are delightfully original top-drawer works of art, using a *crafting* technique that he invented out of obstinacy. (Zero out of ten dentists recommend.)

DOCK ELLIS, PITTSBURGH PIRATES, 2016   JACKIE ROBINSON, BROOKLYN DODGERS, 2013   AARON JUDGE, NEW YORK YANKEES, 2019

And the good news is, much like an "As Seen on TV" commercial, that's not all! When you utilize the part of your astonishing human body that coordinates your brain with your hands, you will actually see positive results cropping up in other aspects of your life. Learning to successfully route robotic wiring or basket weaving can strengthen your general coping skills in navigating traffic or even your relationships with other humans. I think at the heart of this theory is the undeniable value of our capacity for problem-solving. A capacity that loves to be challenged and exercised, as we learn to manipulate our crafting materials into articles of value.

"Value?" you ask. "What value could these small Christmas trees made of clothespins possess? Are you telling me I'll get rich making earrings out of vintage bottlecaps?"

Value is a relative concept. Yes, you may very well make some money from crafting objects that people desire, but to my way of thinking, you also create a substantial value in the act of making things for others (or yourself), and you can multiply that value if you make things *with* others. Any success that I have had as a professional adult must be at least partially attributed to my parents' tendency to make things with me and my siblings. I left their nest and entered the big, scary world with a can-do attitude, knowing that I had a lot left to learn (I still do!).

The most important part that crafting has played in my own life, however, is that it saved me from my own weaker tendencies. I was thrilled to learn that the pleasure I found in solving the puzzles of woodworking actually felt just as fun as playing video games, or engaging in other less productive activities. When I make things with my hands, I feel like I'm playing hooky from the world, but when I'm done, I have a beautiful cutting board or a jewelry box!

And lastly, making things makes one a better citizen. When you learn to pay attention to where your materials are coming from and how they're being produced/harvested, it expands your awareness of the world in general, and how responsibly (or not) everything is being harvested/consumed. You can learn about other makers in your area and form a community that shares tools, materials, and knowledge. This can lead to friendly bartering, and before you know it you'll have swapped a coffee table for a new pair of custom cowboy boots.

The purchase of manufactured goods tends to bolster isolation, especially nowadays, when you can get darn near anything delivered to your doorstep. On the other hand, engaging in the world of crafting fosters a sense of affection for one's neighborhood, whether it's for the people or for the materials available locally. Talk is cheap, and actions speak louder than words, so it's hard to deny the time and care involved in anything you can make. It's the difference between a handmade card, however clumsy, and a store-bought sentiment. I have said it before and I'll say it again: In all varieties, making things is a great way to say "I love you."

INTRODUCTION

BY DAYNA ISOM JOHNSON

You are a maker.

Yeah, you read that right.

As adults, many of us have unfortunately strayed away from our inherent creativity. Instead, we fall victim to thoughts like "I'm not creative," "I could never make anything," or "Crafting is for kids." We are constantly putting down or flat-out denying our creative skills. In today's society of smartphones, tablets, and relentless workweeks, we have abandoned the activity that once brought us so much joy: making.

What happened to the papier-mâché master inside of us? The beaded bracelet boss? The egg crate creative expert? Let's wake that kid up! We are born makers; now it's time for you to rediscover what making can bring to your life.

Still too scared to pick up the hot glue gun?

Consider the fact that aside from challenging your creativity, making can ease stress. It can nurture new friendships, revive old ones, and reignite the sparks of artistry that have been lying dormant within you.

Remember the sense of accomplishment that you felt as a seven-year-old who just completed your first macaroni necklace? The joy and pride you felt when you showed it to your mom or dad?

Making means envisioning a world limited only by imagination, and then using every drop of magic inside us to bring it to life.

Sometimes, the world delivers something far beyond anything you could have imagined.

I remember the day I received the call inviting me to be a part of *Making It*. It was August 22, 2017: exactly three weeks after I'd walked into the towering 30 Rockefeller Plaza for an in-person audition with the producers of the show, including the one and only Amy Poehler, via video conference. I was so incredibly hyped about the potential to be a part of a positive show shining a light on the maker community I love so much.

I had convinced myself that if I was able to land this, it wouldn't be much different from my 9-to-5 at Etsy as the Trend Expert, working with, learning from, and highlighting makers and crafters from around the globe. Except this job would be viewed by millions of people on a major network (terrified!).

My husband, Ryan, and I were at baggage claim in the Miami airport when my phone rang. We'd just gotten back from a trip to Paris, where I'd done my very best to stop worrying about the chance of a lifetime. A few days before the phone call, I told Ryan that I was officially giving this up to the universe, and if it was meant to be then it would be. I would no longer stress or think I wasn't good enough to judge some of the most talented crafters in the United States.

But here we were. And the phone was ringing. The caller ID showed my colleague's name.

I said to myself, "I'm on vacation, this must be something serious for her to call me."

I answered, and in the calmest voice you can imagine, she said, "You got it. Filming starts in three weeks. Pack your bags, you're going to Los Angeles."

And just like that, I lost my damn mind. I proceeded to run laps around the baggage claim all while dropping the most F-bombs one person could possibly say and internally bursting with gratitude, excitement, and fear all wrapped up in one.

From day one of filming, Amy, Nick, and all the tremendous producers made it very clear that *Making It* was going to be a show of positivity. One that would bring delight and fun to prime-time TV. It was going to be a show for families and friends to enjoy together. It would spark memories, inspire creativity, and, of course, make you laugh.

The makers would put their personal spin on challenges each week while Amy and Nick would encourage them. Simon and I would take on the role of bad guys (in the nicest way possible) and send a maker home after each master craft. Simon would bring his lens of more than thirty-five years in the window dressing business, and I would offer makers my perspective of working with successful artists from Etsy.

I believe that one of the many reasons viewers love *Making It* is because it takes you back to your childhood. When Khiem created his dream rocket ship playhouse, how many of us remembered building our first fort?

How many of us remembered our absolute favorite Halloween costume after watching Jo take home the gold for her sock puppet monster?

As children, we were all makers. We were excited and proud to show off what we made. There was no judgment, no pressure, and we never shrank away from the places our imaginations would lead us.

Take a walk down memory lane with me and think back to your early memories of crafting. Is it the strong scent of gooey rubber cement, braiding friendship bracelets, or painstakingly gluing ice pop sticks into the fort or log cabin of your dreams?

When you made something, you felt a sense of accomplishment. You were able to complete a project from start to finish and show off your fancy creations.

Mom's refrigerator door turned into the Metropolitan Museum of Art. We were makers. We were creative. We had an imagination. And then we became grown-ups.

Being a maker, to me, means taking risks. It means allowing yourself to be free. It means getting your hands dirty and not giving a damn.

It does not mean being an expert. It does not mean making money from the items you make. It's about practicing patience, offering yourself quality time, and being proud of something you created with your own hands.

Making It is reawakening the roots of our crafting skills. It shows us that we can all be makers again. Now put down your phone and . . . make It!

WHAT IS CRAFTING AND WHY ARE SO MANY PEOPLE DOING IT?

Creativity lives in all of us, and there's no better way to express yourself than by making something by hand. From food to gifts to home décor to clothing—any number of ideas can be made better by adding a piece of YOU through making. And this practice is so much more than just a hobby—it's a global phenomenon.

When people talk about crafting it probably conjures a specific image for you. Maybe it's knitting a sweater or crocheting a blanket. It could be sewing an apron. It could be weaving on a loom. Or maybe you're a seasoned crafter, and it's building your own dining room table from a hundred-year-old oak tree or making your own bespoke candles from beeswax—who knows! That's the best part about crafting—there's something for everyone, and we're sure there's something for you, too. One of the great things about making is the aspirational element, the fact that anyone can do it.

So, how do you get started? What's the right craft for you to excel at? The best thing you can do is just start, and if starting scares you, we've got the perfect list of faster crafts to get your glue-gunning muscles nice and limber. Whether you like miniature versions of things like terrariums, or you want to make a floor-to-ceiling party backdrop, we believe that not only can you do it, but you definitely should.

Out of this idea and the desire to add a bit more fun, a bit more heart, and a lot more glitter to weeknight TV, *Making It* was born on NBC. At a time when everything felt dark and there was meanness on just about every channel, the need for a show that brought warmth and light and joy to the airwaves was not only a necessity, but a balm. And so Amy Poehler and Nick Offerman rolled up their sleeves and got to making. With a new crew of Makers each season, they tackled projects both challenging and fun to create lasting memories and, honestly, some pretty cool stuff. As Makers, each contestant brought their unique craft to the table, showcasing a wide variety of talents and tastes. It wasn't just easy to get absorbed in this competition—it was impossible not to.

Making It has provided viewers with inspiration for a number of reasons, not least of which is the spirit of encouragement conveyed by every participant, judge, and host. It embodies the spirit of crafting that draws so many people to knit sweaters, quilt blankets, build canoes, and sew Halloween costumes. Making things connects people—there's a universality to it that gives makers a sense of belonging. So your friend who prefers to work with felt and your coworker who specializes in balloons are both on the same team. And it's one that probably has really cool hand-bedazzled uniforms that we want you to feel inspired to wear whenever you want.

So, whether you're more than adept with a handsaw and a drill or you've no idea how to paint a wall, there's something in this book for you. We've filled these pages not only with projects, but with plenty of craft puns and encouragement to help keep you going when things get tough. There may be craft fails—and that's okay. Always be open to change; if it seems like your vision isn't coming to life, continue to adjust and experiment. That's half the fun! Creativity is all about what you want to make/do/see/be. And the sky's the limit; dreaming big—even if you're working medium—is the whole point.

ABOUT THIS BOOK

In this book you'll find a number of projects that were inspired by the Makers who encourage us to leave the TV off (after the episode, of course) and get to making. On the show, we see paper crafters work with wood and felt, and woodworkers get their hands dirty with Mod Podge. It feels great to watch people make things from scratch, right in front of us, with their bare hands. And the best part is knowing that we (you!) can do it, too.

There are both Faster Crafts—to help ease you into this new world of crafting and refresh your memory on what exactly an eyelet puncher is, and that can be completed while watching an episode of the show—and Master Crafts—designed to test your skills and creativity, but hopefully not your patience.

We're sure there's something for everyone here, but don't let the craft puns and puppy photos fool you—this book isn't for the *paint* of heart. . . . We're just kidding, crafting is supposed to be exactly that—fun! Prepare to get your hands, your apron, and your work surface dirty (we also offer up some handy cleaning and tidying tips along the way).

So get ready, Makers, and let's make it!

A CRAFTER'S PANTRY

BASIC CRAFT SUPPLIES

Depending on what you want to make and what type of crafting you want to do, you'll need different tools and supplies. But there are a few general items that are great for a number of projects, and some you most likely already have. We've outlined a selection of the more basic items to pack your craft pantry with, so they're ready whenever you may need them. Just hang up your pegboard and dust off your storage bins, and let's stock your craft pantry!

ADHESIVES

We all know Elmer's, but there's a wide world of glue beyond that elementary school staple. Here are some adhesives that we think are good to have on hand so you don't find yourself in a *sticky* situation.

HOT GLUE: Hot glue is indispensable in almost all areas of craft. You can use hot glue for myriad projects and it will never let you down. Tip: Hot glue takes a while to dry, but if you have a can of compressed air you can use that to freeze the hot glue so that it dries faster, allowing you to move on with your project.

GLUE DOTS: These handy, single pieces of glue that you apply with a specialized dispenser work more like adhesive putty. Great for precise application, without some of the mess that comes with more liquid adhesives.

ADHESIVE SPRAY: Glue in a can! Not as silly as it sounds, this spray application of an adhesive is great for woodworking and beyond, as it allows for a thin coating that's virtually impossible to unstick.

WOOD GLUE: Right there in the name itself: You'll want wood glue ready and available when you're woodworking, as an alternative (and complementary) option to staples and nails.

CA GLUE: More commonly referred to as super or crazy glue. This stuff is not messing around—great for repairs and a number of other jobs, but use with care, as this is difficult to unstick by design.

MOD PODGE: Sort of the holy grail of craft products. It's wildly useful, as it's not only a glue but an all-in-one glue, sealer, and finish. This stuff is amazing, and you'd be hard pressed to find a replacement when a project calls for it.

Beyond what's mentioned here, there're also glue sticks, material-specific glue (such as for leather, suede, and glass), extra-strength versions, and a variety of sealants. You don't need to have it all, but having a baseline of adhesives like what we've outlined here is a strong starting point.

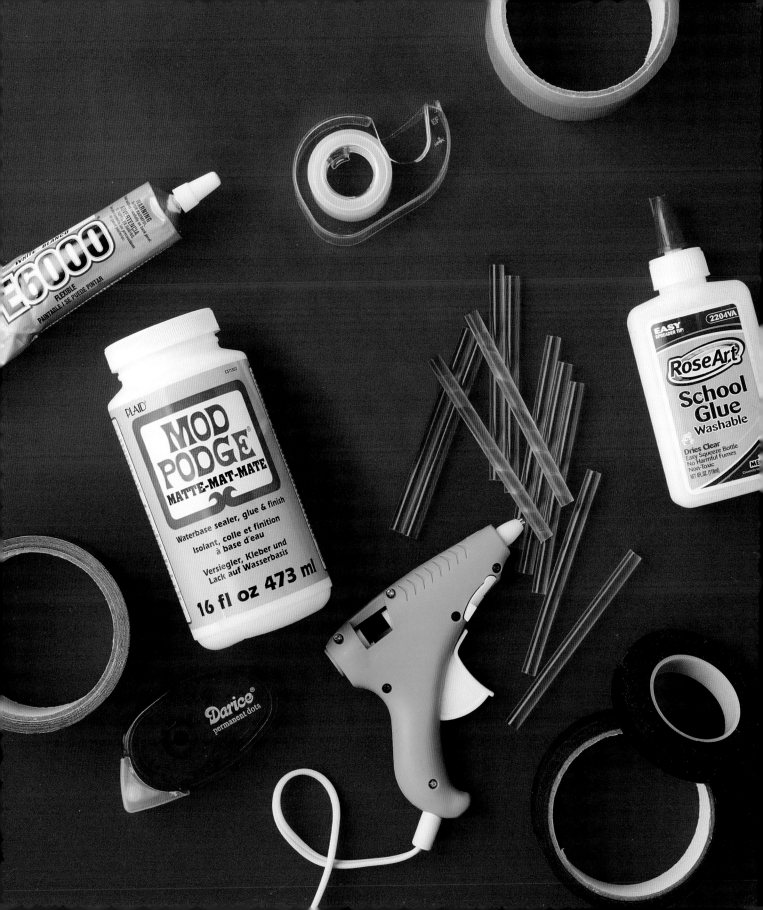

TAPE

You probably know that you can find it in one-sided or two-, but there are more tape types out there than you ever thought possible! Here are a few we find it helpful to have around the house.

PAINTER'S TAPE: Beyond just preventing paint from getting on your baseboards or crown molding, painter's tape is great for crafting as it's easily removable and leaves no residue.

UTILITY TAPE: Who knew that duct tape came in so many different colors?! Expand your horizons beyond the familiar gray and have this household staple at the ready as you get started crafting.

MASKING TAPE: Another familiar option that works great and stays on most surfaces pretty well.

INVISIBLE TAPE: Of course! The staple, the OG, the tape everyone has and knows and uses, maybe daily? No explanation required, we bet there's already some in a drawer nearby right now . . .

FLORAL TAPE: A great item to keep on hand for working with floral arrangements, both fresh and paper alike. Useful for keeping stems together and wrapping wire, too. This tape works a little differently: You'll need to stretch it in order to activate the stickiness.

WASHI TAPE: A decorative, masking-like tape that is durable, flexible, and available in a variety of widths, textures, patterns, and colors. It tears easily and is generally used to add visual interest to a project.

SAFETY GEAR

Before we get further into the tools and materials, we need to cover safety gear and its importance in crafting. The below items are great to have, but depending on what you're making you might need other safety gear, such as a fire extinguisher. You should always ask yourself two questions when using a new material for a project: Could this burst into flame? And would it be cool if it did? But seriously, you might want to keep a fire extinguisher around just in case.

SAFETY GOGGLES: Given the choice, a pair of safety goggles looks a whole lot better than an eye patch, both on and off.

WAX EARPLUGS OR BAND-STYLE PROTECTION EARMUFFS: The only reason to not listen to advice to wear ear protection is because you're already wearing ear protection and can't hear the instructions.

FACE MASK: In particular, while working with paint, certain adhesives, varnishes, or sealants, be mindful of harmful fumes. Open a window, work outdoors whenever possible, and have a face mask on hand to block your nose and mouth.

RUBBER OR LATEX GLOVES: Especially when dyeing, and with many other projects, gloves will protect your hands (and therefore your face, mouth, eyes, etc.) from turning a very bright shade of blue—or pink, red, orange, yellow . . . you get the idea.

TOOLS

The tools that you need will vary widely depending on what projects you want to do, but below are a few of the basics that you may already be familiar with and that are good to have at the ready.

TAPE MEASURE: Measure twice, and then measure a third time, and cut once.

HAMMER: You know, for hammering things, like nails, drywall anchors, and sometimes your worktable when things aren't going the way you want.

NEEDLE-NOSE PLIERS: For working small.

LONG-NOSE PLIERS: For working even smaller.

MAGNETIC LEVEL: A level is like a diet—it doesn't have to be perfect, but it should be balanced.

SCREWDRIVER: Both flathead and Phillips.

STAPLE GUN: You know, for stapling things.

GLUE GUN: For the truly necessary hot glue that we mentioned before.

SHARP OBJECTS

From scissors to to X-Acto knives, there are a number of sharp tools to serve your precise needs. As with any and all sharp objects, safety always comes first, so be sure to familiarize yourself with each tool and its proper usage and instructions before using.

SCISSORS: These handy tools come in all shapes and sizes, and range from kitchen scissors to fabric shears. Source what's right for your project, but mostly your average household scissors will do nicely.

SELF-RETRACTING UTILITY KNIFE: Otherwise known as box cutters, these sharp tools come with built-in safety mechanisms to help ensure injury-free usage.

X-ACTO KNIFE: X-Acto knives are extremely useful given their pointed, precision tip that allows for very *exact* cuts.

CRAFT CUTTING MACHINES: Craft cutting machines like a Silhouette are designed to cut materials such as paper, vinyl, or fabric into your desired shape using specialized design software. They are great for cutting intricate designs with precision or for cutting in large quantities.

Beyond the tools here there's even more: rotary cutters, precision razors, guillotine paper cutters, cutting pliers, wire cutters, and don't even get us started on saws. Be sure to research what bonus tools you might need before buying them, as this is a solid starting set. Tip: A self-healing cutting mat is a great investment and will spare your other surfaces unwanted nicks and scrapes.

SOME OTHER ITEMS THAT
MIGHT COME IN HANDY

These are less mandatory, but you'll be glad you have them, and most likely you already do, or can find them with relative ease. You won't use all of these with every project, but when you need to draw out an idea before executing, you'll be glad you have a sketchpad or notebook at the ready; or when you need a small piece of cardboard to back a framed piece, it'll be good that you kept that leftover shipping box.

FINE-TIP PERMANENT MARKER	**HIGHLIGHTERS**
PENCILS	**MARKERS**
ERASERS	**RULER**
COLORED PENCILS	**HOLE PUNCH**
CRAYONS	**SKETCHPAD**

TEXTILES

Fiber crafts is one of the largest areas of crafting, with materials and techniques that span a wide range of projects and possibilities and often cross over into other areas. Fiber arts is also one of the oldest domains of arts and crafts and uniquely touches all parts of history and culture.

From yarn to cotton to denim to canvas to macramé cord to rope to embroidery thread, there's a wide world of fibers and textiles out there that can enable your wildest DIY dreams. Almost half the projects in this book incorporate textiles in some way, and it's easy to see how essential these versatile materials are to crafting in general.

We'll explore a handful of fiber crafts that will be featured in this book, but the possibilities extend far beyond what we're able to cover here.

MATERIALS

FELT: A textile of condensed fibers, such as wool or acrylic. Felt is one of the most versatile fabrics around when it comes to crafting. You can cover just about anything with felt to decorate or help hide what's beneath—just take a look at the Rainbow Play Tent project (page 131) and see how felt transforms pool noodles and wood slats into a magical rainbow! You can sew felt, glue it, cut it, and fold it into whatever you want it to be. Stuff it with batting for a pillow-like cloud (page 135), or cut out shapes to make felt pizza and tacos (page 99). And with the numerous colors available, there's sure to be enough felt options for whatever your project needs.

MACRAMÉ CORD: Macramé cord offers a number of great options for crafting. With unlimited knot potential, there's a macramé project for every style. We've seen some pretty inspiring projects on this show, from wall hangings to light fixtures (both of which we've re-created here!) and macramé cord can be dyed, extending its potential even further.

ROPE: Similar to macramé cord, rope is a DIY staple. You can wrap plenty of items with rope, as well as paint it, glue it, and tie it.

FABRIC: This covers all manner of materials—think of everything from canvas to linen to denim to cotton to silk. You can sew most fabrics, stitch them, weave them, and paint them. You can even dye fabric to transform neutral materials into vibrant works of art—see for yourself with our Tote Bag with a Twist (page 87).

YARN: Yarn probably calls to mind homemade afghans and comfy scarves, and while yarn is used in all manner of projects, it is most specific to knitting and crochet. It comes in a variety of colors and weights. But think outside the box with yarn: It makes for great tassels you can add to a bag (see page 87), or substitute it for ribbon when wrapping presents.

TECHNIQUES

CROSS-STITCH: From wall hangings to bookmarks, there's a number of fun things to create with cross-stitch—all you need is some embroidery floss, a needle, and aida cloth, an open-weave fabric that's natural mesh makes it perfect for cross-stitch patterns. Create custom designs, lettering, or geometric patterns for your own art pieces, or go big and use a pegboard instead of aida cloth and yarn instead of floss, as we did, for a truly unique piece of art! Check out the Cross-Stitch Wall Art project on page 143 for more on the technique and some tips behind this fun craft.

EMBROIDERY: Similar to cross-stitch, embroidery is a classic craft that's incredibly versatile in its output. You can embroider most fabrics, so everything from T-shirts to jeans to pillow covers to tote bags to patches is open to your interpretation. Embroidery floss comes in a variety of colors, good for both blending in and standing out.

SEWING: Either by hand or with a machine, sewing can result in a number of different outcomes, from clothing to unicorn heads (page 121)! It's just as handy for repairing holes as it is for making quilts, and you can, quite possibly, sew almost any fabric, so the sky is truly the limit here.

PAPER

Paper crafts range from the more obvious options like flowers and origami to using paper to accent other crafts, paint on, cut out, and more. Paper is easy to source, as so much of what's best to work with is readily available at craft stores and even more general stores. There's a lot that can be done with regular construction paper, and branching out into specialty papers opens the doors even more widely.

MATERIALS

Some paper types, and paper-like materials, that you're most likely to need or work with for most DIY projects include:

CARDSTOCK: This is a medium-weight paper that's rather sturdy. You can find any number of colors, textures, and weights (think: thickness) of cardstock, so whatever craft you're making, there's a cardstock for that.

CARDBOARD AND FOAM BOARD: We all know cardboard and likely interact with it on a daily basis. But before it ends up in the recycling bin, there are plenty of great projects where cardboard can assist (see the Food Truck on page 137). Foam board is similar in thickness and usefulness for crafting, but it's a bit more substantial and sturdier than cardboard. So if you need flexibility, cardboard is the way to go. You can paint both, glue them, cut them, and altogether create just about anything.

CONSTRUCTION PAPER: With its many colors, construction paper is useful far beyond the elementary school classroom. It doesn't hurt to have some on hand, as you never know when you might need a paper chain at a moment's notice!

COPY PAPER: Yep, what's currently in your printer can be used for a number of craft projects, too. Who knew?

CREPE PAPER: Great for party streamers, photo backdrops, and paper flowers alike.

KRAFT PAPER: A hard-working paper that's as classic as it gets. Fun to draw or paint on, it's foldable, cuttable, glue-able, and more. And it's a great option for wrapping paper, which you can then decorate yourself.

NEWSPRINT: You know, what shows up on your porch on Sunday mornings and you've recycled by Sunday afternoon? Newsprint can be incredibly useful for papier-mâché projects, or you could save some for gift wrapping—use the comics for a kids' birthday, or real estate for a house warming present.

TISSUE PAPER: For more than just filling gift bags, tissue paper is key when crafting paper flowers.

VELLUM: Very popular for stationery, but also comes up on occasion while crafting. This sheer paper is great when working with photos.

Paper also comes in a variety of finishes. Some papers are metallic, or foil stamped, while others feel textured, like crepe paper, and still others feel smooth, like rice paper. And most papers you can embellish with paint, ink, markers, dyes, and more. Experimenting with different options and finishes can really transform your project.

WOOD

Woodworking is an area of making that typically demands practice, patience, and attention to detail, but you're sure to see great things start to come out of the wood*work*! Wood is a medium that requires problem-solving, inspires creativity, and results in pride in the finished product—plus, it's incredibly fun.

Woodworking is different from carpentry in that it doesn't require that you build or repair large structures, but instead focuses on the process of making smaller pieces like furniture, containers, musical instruments, art pieces, and more from wood. Projects that are hand crafted from a piece of wood have a unique personality that is all their own, and no two are exactly alike due to the nature of wood itself.

MATERIALS

Beginning a woodworking project doesn't necessarily require you to set up a workshop equipped with table saws, sanders, and other (loud!) equipment. Instead, you can ease into this craft by having a few basic tools on hand to get you started. And, until you're ready to take the leap into owning your own power tools, you can rent many of them or have your wood for all the projects you dream up cut at most major home-improvement stores.

Context is key as you embark on your journey into the wonderful world of wood-working. Every wood has its advantages, and which wood is right for your project depends on the end goal. The same goes for tools. Rounded corners will require a miter saw, while a jigsaw is best for shapes. Wood glue is often useful, but certain projects only need staples.

And then there's the finished look. Wood is beautiful in its own right, but there are many options to enhance the wood's natural features: varnish, shellac, lacquer, beeswax, paste wax, oil-based polyurethane, water-based polyurethane, tung oil, linseed oil, walnut oil, safflower oil, Danish oil . . . It's likely if you're following a specific set of instructions that it will come with its own recommendations, but get creative and experiment. Linseed oil will look different from one wood type to the next, as will all the other finishing options.

Just remember that selecting the right materials is essential to a job well done. And safety is paramount when working with the various saws and other tools that are a given with woodworking. Holding a handsaw around the shop makes you look like a pro; holding it anywhere else makes you look like a serial killer.

FROM THE WOOD SHOP: JIMMY DIRESTA

I often find that many people who want to get started wood-working or "making" have a tendency to stick to what's easy. And while that's good at the start, to get better at anything it's important to get outside your comfort zone—to challenge yourself with newer, bigger projects, new materials and processes.

A good practice to get outside your comfort zone is to ask a friend or family member if they need something built . . . something you wouldn't have thought to make yourself. With a project like this, you have to build to the specific needs of the "client." This may require learning something you didn't know you needed to learn. Do research and look at examples of others' work in the same area.

One simple thought I often keep in mind when learning something new is, "If he or she can do it, I can do it, too." So go and get uncomfortable and learn something new!

DYES

Dyeing is a fun craft to get into, especially in combination with other areas of craft like textiles and macramé. You can dye any number of materials, such as canvas, rope or cord, linen, cotton, and more. And with techniques like shibori, tie-dye, and dip dyeing, the design potential is huge.

The two different types of dye you can easily work with at home are artificial dyes and natural dyes. In the book, we used artificial dyes for all projects involved, but natural dyes yield similarly great results, and beautiful colors can be made from the most everyday foods.

BEETS: RED

ONION SKIN: ORANGE

SPINACH: GREEN

RED CABBAGE: BLUE

BLUEBERRIES: PURPLE

AVOCADO PITS: PINK

MATERIALS

When mixing and dyeing with both natural and artificial dyes, you should always wear gloves and an apron. Dyes can be pesky, and if you don't take the proper precautions, you might wind up with blue hands for several days thereafter.

Preparing your fabrics for dyeing is equally as important. Most materials that you buy need to be scoured before you dye them. Scouring is a deep clean of the material that allows the dye to really penetrate the fibers. The process is different depending on the type of material you want to work with (e.g., cotton should be treated differently than wool), so be sure to research the correct method beforehand.

TOOLS

You'll need a number of different tools and supplies when dyeing, but some basics include:

RUBBER GLOVES

CLAMPS OR CLOTHESPINS

BUCKET

RUBBER BANDS

STAINLESS STEEL SPOON
OR TONGS

DROP CLOTH

And cleanup is a whole separate story. *Never* use a bucket or pot that you dyed in for anything food related in the future. If you'd like to dye fabrics in your sink, make sure it is made of stainless steel and not fiberglass or porcelain. And make sure you properly wash all dyed fabrics before using them so they won't bleed color where it's not wanted. Read the dye instructions on artificial dyes carefully, and be equally mindful when making natural dyes at home. Don't cut corners—unless you're woodworking something with rounded edges, and in that case, you should use a miter saw.

Canvas

Linen

Cotton

PAINT

You probably started painting in preschool—those finger-painted masterpieces were just the beginning. There's a paint type for every material, so you can paint just about anything from wood to plastic to paper to canvas to fabric. And you can get creative with how you paint; there's a big wide world beyond brushes and rollers! Consider stamping with bunched-up tissue paper for a more textured look, or a plastic fork can be used to create fun designs, like our Fork-Stamped Table Runner on page 63. Feel free to branch out—evergreen tree branches are great for brushing on more abstract, wispy designs!

MATERIALS

ACRYLIC PAINT: Acrylic paint is the godfather of craft paint. In the nineties, your mom most certainly used acrylic paint to paint a pair of friendly snowmen on a piece of wood, and it is still the medium general crafters turn to most when it's time to get their paint on. Acrylic paint is created with an emulsion of water, so it is considered a "water-based" paint, rather than an "oil-based" paint. Acrylic paint works well for paper, wood, canvas, metal, Styrofoam, resin, terra-cotta and more! Plus, acrylics are a great foundational paint to mix with a formulated medium for things like marbling, fabric painting, or when you are looking for a matte finish.

WATERCOLOR PAINT: Watercolor isn't only for painting scenes of koi ponds and waterways in Venice—it can transform a plain surface into something stunning. Makers use watercolors to make everything from greeting cards to Easter eggs to coasters come alive with color. Watercolor paints are water-based, so they offer gorgeous transparency and tinting. They are also a wonderful way to introduce kids to painting because they are relatively low mess (note: We said *relatively*).

CHALK PAINT: If you have a love of farmhouse chic, you are likely familiar with chalk paint, a staple when attempting a modern, rustic look. Chalk paints have an ultra-matte finish and are great for furniture and home décor. Plus, they are multi-surface paints that can be used on decorative glass, furniture, cabinets, and walls. Chalk paints can be sanded and distressed and are generally finished with a wax to seal the paint and provide a smooth protective finish. (Note: This is not the same as chalkboard paint; you'll need a chalkboard medium or actual chalkboard paint to make an at-home blackboard.)

FABRIC PAINT: From puffy paint to silk screening, there are so many interesting methods for painting fabric. Fabric paint can be used to hand paint, stamp, stencil, or spray a design on fabric or clothing, and it can hold up to a washing machine so that it can be worn or used again and again. Many fabric paints also include a medium that makes them softer on fabric than acrylic paint, which can feel crunchy on fabric.

SPRAY PAINT: Spray paint is a big Maker favorite because it can evenly cover just about any surface. Plus, spray paints are ideal for painting trickier surfaces that may have crevices or corners that a brush can't reach. It's available in a number of finishes and has the unique ability to make old things look fresh and new!

TOOLS

Painting requires tools that go beyond brushes. Here are some handy items to have around as you get started painting, stamping, and more.

PAINTBRUSHES . . . DUH	**PAINT STIRRERS**
FOAM BRUSHES	**DROP CLOTHS**
PAINT ROLLERS	**PAINTER'S TAPE**
PAINT PANS	**PAINT SCRAPER**

FASTER CRAFTS

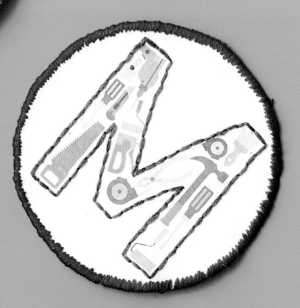

MASTER MAKER PATCHES

What better reward for a job well done than a patch! At the end of each of the *Making It* challenges, the winning Maker was awarded a patch to wear as a crafty badge of honor—luckily, you don't have to go on a crafting competition show to earn your own. This simple method for patch making doesn't require any special sewing skills, which is great news for us non-sewers who *needle* the help we can get! Plus, once your patches are done you can stick them on a jacket, backpack, or apron to show the world you've made it! Have fun choosing your own designs for this project.

SUPPLIES

Your patch designs

Printer

Printable heat-transfer vinyl for dark fabrics

Scissors

Canvas

Dish towel or napkin

Iron

Embroidery floss in red, yellow, and orange

Needle

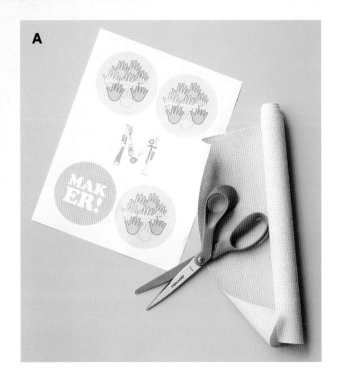

A

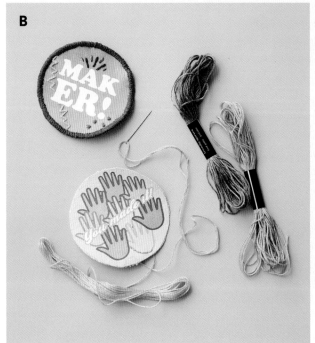

B

1. Print the desired patch design on printable heat-transfer vinyl. (PHOTO A)

2. Using scissors, cut around the design to remove excess vinyl.

3. Peel off the backing and place the heat-transfer vinyl circle on top of the canvas and cover with a dish towel.

4. Press the heat-transfer circle with a hot, dry iron for 15–20 seconds.

5. Remove the dish towel and check to make sure the vinyl has fully adhered to the canvas. If any edges are lifting, reapply the dish towel and press again with the iron for a few seconds.

6. Once the vinyl is fully adhered to the canvas, cut around the design on your canvas.

7. Using embroidery floss and a needle, stitch around the perimeter of the patch to create a dense loop. If desired, stitch on top of the design to add dimension. (PHOTO B)

8. Attach to a jacket, bag, etc., by sewing, gluing, or using Heat n Bond.

MAKER SPOTLIGHT: REBECCA PROPES

From the time I was itty-bitty, I have always loved to create. In fact, my weekly trips to the elementary school library were driven by the desire to check out the latest in "Make & Do" books, so my career in design and DIY is no surprise.

When I was finishing high school, the thought of pursuing a career in the arts never crossed my mind. I spent some time exploring different degrees, until I started listening to myself and chose to go back to school and enroll in an interior design program. Creating was something I always felt moved to do but never truly understood what a gift it was. Creating is a way to explore, grow, and inspire.

People always tell me that they have zero creativity, but I think it's about finding the one thing you love and sticking with it. Creating is about making mistakes, and trying again to find what works. Creating is making one hundred sketches to get to that OMG moment. Creating is about letting go and leaning into a thought that can turn into something awesome!

I think my use of color and layering of patterns and textures helped make my projects successful on the show. There were definitely takeaways from every challenge, but the Staycation Shed was for sure a favorite! It was a totally stripped-down shed transformation, inside and out. This wasn't just basic crafting; this was schematics, sketches, concepts, design, building, and DIYs to overhaul the space. This is the hardest I have ever been pushed but for sure was the most rewarding experience.

The ability to tackle such a big project didn't come overnight, but it did come, with trial, error, and not being afraid to jump in with both feet. So if there is any advice I can give to those ready to start their journey into the creative arts, it's to take the leap, make the mistakes, and find the "thing" that makes you do a happy dance!

PIÑATA PARTY
FAVORS/INVITATIONS

〰〰〰〰〰〰〰〰〰

Our Makers made some very clever 3-D invitations during one Faster Craft challenge, inspiring these fun and fruity piñata party invites! These mini piñatas are made from paper plates and can be stuffed with a message and delivered as an invitation, or filled with treats and handed out as favors. Instructions here are for a watermelon design, but feel free to select your favorites and make oranges, lemons, or even dragonfruit! No matter what, they are sure to be a total hit (no baseball bat required!).

SUPPLIES

Scissors

7-inch (18-cm) paper plates

Hot glue gun filled with glue

Confetti, candy, and/or invitations/messages for filling

Crepe and/or tissue paper in red and green

Black cardstock

1. Using scissors, cut the paper plates in half. (PHOTO A)

2. Place a line of hot glue on the rounded edge of one of the paper plates and press it against the matching side of the other half of the plate to connect. This should create a half circle with a pocket in the middle.

3. Fill the pocket of the piñata with confetti, candy, and/or an invitation or message.

4. Glue a sheet of crepe paper over the pocket to close it. Use scissors to remove excess paper.

5. Cut the crepe paper into 1-inch (2.5-cm) strips (strips for both the rind color and the fruit color), then cut ¼-inch-deep (6-mm) snips into the strips to create fringe. (PHOTO B)

6. Starting at the curved end of the piñata and working toward the top, glue the fringe strips onto the plate, starting with the rind color and changing colors after the rind or peel of the fruit is completed.

7. Continue until the paper plate is completely covered with fringe.

8. Once the piñata is fully covered, use scissors (or a craft cutting machine) to cut out additional details for the fruit out of the card stock (i.e., seeds, slices, etc.).

9. Apply the additional details to the piñatas using hot glue.

TIP: A craft cutting machine is helpful when cutting small pieces, like the seeds, or more intricate pieces, like the slices.

TIP: Tissue and crepe paper are thin and hot glue is hot, which can be a painful combination when you enter skin into the equation. If you are interested in holding on to your fingerprints, consider using protective silicone finger caps (super cheap on Amazon!) to protect your digits while you're working with the hot stuff.

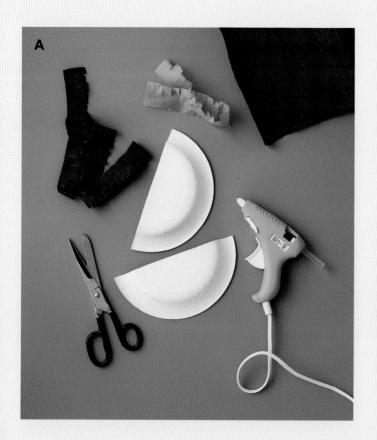

FORK-STAMPED
TABLE RUNNER

You don't need a fancy craft room with ox-hair paintbrushes and high-viscosity paint in bespoke hues to make something beautiful. In fact, if you've got some leftover plastic forks from last weekend's BBQ, we've got a project to make your table look terrific! This table runner is stamped with fabric paint using plastic forks, and let us just say, it's pretty forkin' great.

SUPPLIES

Fabric paint in 4 different colors (red, yellow, pink, purple)

4 plastic forks with flat bottoms (one fork per color used)

Paintbrush

Cotton table runner, prewashed

Eyelets

Eyelet setter

Embroidery floss to match paint colors

Scissors

1. Apply an even amount of paint on the bottom of the first fork using a paintbrush.

2. Press the fork into one corner of the table runner, using even pressure.

3. Apply the next color of paint on the second fork and stamp the table runner again, next to the first stamp, alternating the direction of the fork (horizontally, then vertically, and so on). (PHOTO A)

4. Repeat the process with the third and fourth paint colors and forks.

5. Working from one end of the runner to the other, fill the entire runner with stamps following the above sequence, then let the paint dry completely.

6. Using an eyelet setter, set evenly spaced eyelets on the short edges of the runner and tie on the tassels. (PHOTO B)

7. MAKE THE TASSELS: Without unraveling the skein, gently pull out two 10-inch (25-cm) pieces of embroidery floss and cut with scissors.

8. Lay the skein flat and cut the two looped ends of the skein with scissors, leaving a straight, flat bundle of floss.

9. Wrap one of the 10-inch (25-cm) pieces of floss around the center of the floss bundle. Secure with a double knot.

10. Lift the tassel by the knot and fold the ends of the skein down, with the knot at the top.

11. Take the second piece of 10-inch (25-cm) floss and wrap it around the floss bundle, about ¼ inch (6 mm) from the top. Secure with a double knot and cut excess string from the knot.

12. Trim the ends of the tassel bottom with scissors to make them straight and even.

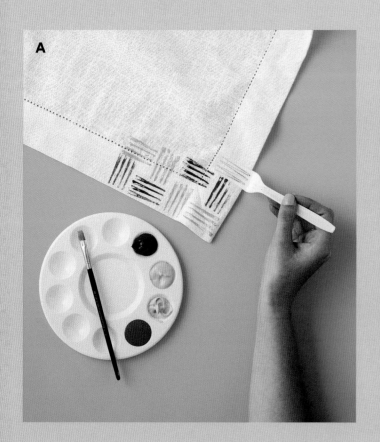

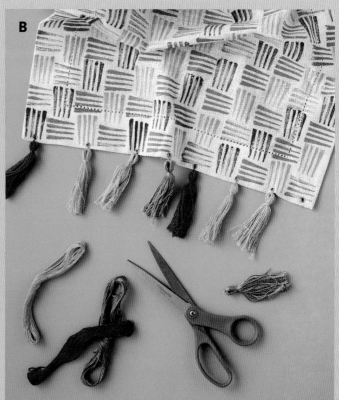

PAPER FLORAL
CENTERPIECE

From construction to crepe and vellum to vinyl, working with paper is a Maker must. And while paper may seem like the most basic of the supplies in your craft room, it can be folded, rolled, bent, and shaped to create innumerable projects. This paper floral centerpiece uses card stock, floral wire, and a little glue to make beautiful blooms, all without a stop at the flower shop.

SUPPLIES

Cardstock in various colors (lavender, peach, pink, yellow, green)

Flower pattern pieces (see pages 184-185)

Scissors

Hot glue gun filled with glue

Pencil

Floral wire

Floral foam

Utility knife

Vase

1. Using cardstock in the colors shown in the photo, cut out the flowers according to the patterns with scissors. (PHOTO A)

2. **MAKE THREE CAGES:** Make a cage-like form to build Flower 1 using the L- shaped template piece A that has 4 strips of paper on one end. Begin by connecting long ends together, securing with a dot of glue to make a circle on the base, with the 4 strips pointing up. Curve the first of the strips pointing up down toward the circular base, and attach to the base using a dot of glue. Repeat until all 4 strips have been folded over and attached to the circular base, revealing a cage-like form. Make the remaining two.

3. **MAKE THREE OF FLOWER 1:** Once the cages have been made, begin rolling the flower petals of all Flower 1-B pieces around a pencil to add dimension. Glue two Flower 1-B blossoms, offset, on top of one another using a dot of hot glue. Glue one Flower 1-C piece in the center of a pair of 1-B blossoms. Repeat the process until all the blossoms are assembled, enough

to cover the cage. Glue the blossoms onto the paper cage using hot glue, distributing them evenly to avoid empty spaces. (PHOTO B)

4. **MAKE FIVE OF FLOWER 2 AND SIX OF FLOWER 3:** Working from the tip of the petal and moving to the center, gently roll the flower petals of Flower 2-A around a pencil, one by one, to create dimension. (PHOTO C) Place a dot of hot glue in the center of the Flower 2-A piece and place a 2-B piece on top. Repeat the process with petal pieces of Flower 2-C through G, arranging them from largest to smallest and ending with the smallest pieces in the center of each flower, in a contrasting color if desired. (PHOTO D)

5. **MAKE THE FOUR GREENERY STEMS:** Gently curl the leaves of the branches around a pencil lengthwise, working one by one. Cut a piece of floral wire to the length of the stem that connects the leaves. Attach the stem to the wire using hot glue. If your stem is thin, apply a dot of glue to the

CONTINUED ➡

E

F

inner edge of the leaves, instead of to the stem, to attach the wire. Repeat with the remaining stems.

6 Choose the desired height for the rest of your flower arrangement. Cut pieces of floral wire to this height (plus ½ inch [12 mm]) using scissors—one piece for each flower.

7 Attach all the flowers to the wire using hot glue. To do this, bend the top ½ inch (12 mm) of the wire and place the bent section flat against the back of the flower. Secure with a generous amount of hot glue. (PHOTO E)

8 Cut the floral foam to fit the size of the desired vase using scissors or a utility knife. Place the foam in the vase.

9 Arrange the flowers and greenery in the vase by sticking the wire in the foam. (PHOTO F)

MAKER SPOTLIGHT: JAMIE HUDSON

My path to craft meandered more than most—through chemistry, physics, and business, pursuits not well known for creative expression. Things got weird when my artist wife and I made a New Year's resolution to be "less boring," to spend less time watching life and more time participating in it. Bit by bit, we turned a handshake agreement, some hobby tools, and the silliest of ideas into an unlikely second career. It's been a barrel ride over a waterfall, and we probably should have learned some lessons along the way. Instead, here is some unsolicited advice for anybody nervous about putting themselves out there.

Fail forward. Failure is a by-product of trying new things and taking chances—do it more. It doesn't matter that the project you made is now glued to your forehead; it matters that you learned how to remove glue with warm, soapy water.

Make more things—make things for others, make things to sell, make things for yourself, and definitely make things because it's fun. Even when things are difficult, find the fun. Tip: It's impossible to stay mad when googly eyes are involved.

Be a fan of your work. Heap praise on yourself like a parent praises their five-year-old's macaroni masterpiece. See the potential, be proud of the progress, then pin it to your refrigerator for all to see. You did good. You made something with your opposable thumbs other than thumbprints on a smartphone. Stan yourself, superstar.

The world is your craft store. Tongue depressors, pipe cleaners, and cotton balls all had dreary careers before becoming craft staples. Crafting is about creating and problem-solving with the tools and materials available in your environment.

Influence yourself. The world is awash in inspiration. Drink it all in and feel inspired, then spit it back out and find your own voice. Never compare your project with anybody else's. Take all the feedback and all the advice you can get, then carefully ignore it.

CONFETTI BANNER

Everyone loves a little confetti at a party . . . until it's time to clean up. That's why we are big fans of this confetti banner. The use of foam tape in this project allows the confetti to move and shake like confetti should, but helps you avoid finding stray confetti in your hair until the end of time.

SUPPLIES

White cardstock

Scissors or craft cutting machine

Colored cardstock

Plastic sheet protectors

Hot glue gun filled with glue

Foam tape

Confetti

Eyelets

Eyelet setter

String

1. Choose a phrase for your banner.

2. Cut out the shape of the first letter from white cardstock, using scissors or a craft cutter.

3. Cut out the outline of the same letter from colored cardstock, using scissors or a craft cutting machine. (PHOTO A)

4. Using scissors, cut around the edge of the sheet protector to make two plastic sheets.

5. Cut pieces of foam tape to fit around the full perimeter of the white cardstock letter shape. Using foam tape allows for space between the cardstock and the plastic, so that the confetti can move and shake around the inside.

6. Remove one side of the foam tape backing and tape pieces to the white cardstock letter shape, leaving the space at the top open and the remaining tape off to the side. Trim tape as needed to ensure there are no gaps.

7. Remove the other side of the foam tape backing and tape the single sheet protector to the white cardstock letter shape. You have now created a pocket to place the confetti in. Cut out the sheet protector around the letter shape. (PHOTO B)

8. Pour confetti into the letter, using the opening between the plastic and the white cardstock letter top. Once it's filled, add a final piece of foam tape to secure the top of the pocket. (PHOTO C)

9. Using hot glue, attach the colored cardstock letter outline to the top of the sheet protector, ensuring all edges align with the white cardstock letter shape on the bottom. The letters are layered as: white cardstock shape, foam tape, confetti, plastic, top colored letter outline.

10. Using an eyelet setter, set two eyelets at the top of the letter. (PHOTO D)

11. Repeat steps 2–10 until all the letters for the desired phrase are completed.

12. Thread string through the eyelets and hang the banner.

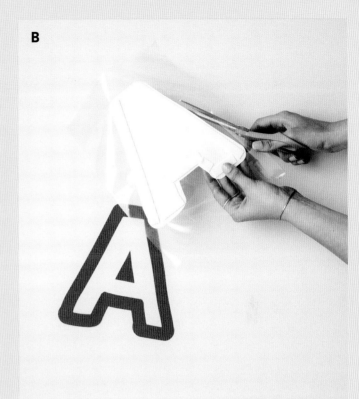

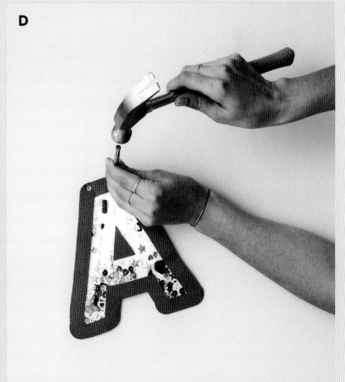

HOMETOWN
TERRARIUM

A traditional terrarium is a miniature garden landscape in a glass container—anything from a fish bowl to a coffee pot to a brandy snifter. Planting a terrarium can feel like building your own little world without having to do any heavy lifting. Plus, by adding whimsical figurines or meaningful trinkets, it can become a tiny glass oasis that is uniquely yours. Makers were challenged to create a terrarium that included elements representative of their hometown to make it their own.

SUPPLIES

2 pounds (905 g) white gravel

1 gallon (3.8 L) wide-mouth glass jar

Horticultural charcoal (if using live plants)

2 pounds (905 g) small stones

Potting soil

3-4 small plants or succulents (living or artificial)

Wooden dinosaur figurine or other decorative item(s)

1 Pour the gravel in the base of the jar. (PHOTO A)

2 Create a small depression in the middle of the gravel and fill the hole with 1 inch (2.5 cm) of horticultural charcoal. (This will keep your terrarium fresh if you are using live plants.)

3 Pour the stones into the jar. (PHOTO B)

4 Add potting soil to the jar until the terrarium is about half full. (PHOTO C)

5 Plant the succulents and plants. (PHOTO D)

6 Add the wooden dinosaur or other desired decorative item(s).

7 Water terrarium every 3 to 6 weeks, or when the soil is dry.

~~~~~~~~~~~~~~~~~~~~~~~~~~~~~~~~~~~~

TIP: When choosing a container for your terrarium, make sure you look for one that will easily magnify sunlight (like clear glass). This will keep your plants nice and toasty and help your terrarium tenants thrive!

SHIBORI PILLOWS

SHED HACK!

Shibori is a Japanese dyeing technique that is anything but shi-boring! In fact, it is so addictive you'll find yourself dyeing every piece of white fabric in your home a deep indigo and creating patterns using traditional shibori techniques. There are endless binding possibilities (rubber bands! rope! paper clips! wood!) for creating different shapes and patterns (stripes! triangles! starbursts! florals!), and the results are sure to be one of a kind.

SUPPLIES

Indigo fabric dye kit or synthetic indigo dye kit

Bucket

Canvas pillow covers, prewashed

Square wooden coasters (one pair for each pillow cover)

Rubber bands

Rubber or latex gloves

Iron

Scissors

Roving yarn or a bulkier, chunky yarn in cream

Embroidery floss in navy

Embroidery needle

1. Prepare the dye according to the package directions. We recommend preparing it in a bucket that you don't mind discoloring, or in a stainless steel sink. We do not recommend dyeing in a porcelain or fiberglass sink.

2. Fold one of the pillow covers like an accordion, lengthwise, to create a long rectangle with one of the short sides facing you.

3. Next, fold the bottom-right corner of the cover over to meet the long side of the rectangle, creating a triangle. Then, continue to fold the canvas into triangles, accordian style, until you have a single small triangle, using all the fabric. (PHOTO A)

4. Sandwich the folded triangle of fabric between the wooden coasters and wrap the packet securely with three to five rubber bands. Repeat steps 1–4 to make more fabric triangles.

5. **DYE THE PILLOW COVERS:**
   To achieve a triangle dye pattern: Fully submerge the triangle bundle in the prepared bucket of dye and allow the fabric to soak according to the package directions, or until you have achieved your optimal shade.

   To achieve a line pattern: While wearing gloves, submerge the bottom half of the triangle in the dye, keeping the top corner dry. Soak the submerged side according to package directions, or until you have achieved your optimal shade.

6. Remove the bundle from the dye bath and rinse in a bucket or stainless steel sink until the water runs clear. (PHOTO B)

7. Remove the rubber bands and coasters, unfold the fabric, and let the pillow covers dry completely. Once dry, remove the wrinkles with a warm iron.

CONTINUED ➡

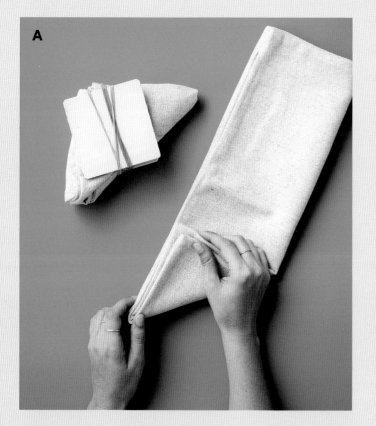

A

B

C

TIP: Dyeing, with either synthetic or natural dyes, is a finicky business. No two dye jobs will be the same— and that's the fun! Longer soak times will lead to richer colors, so be sure to experiment with fabric scraps to get your desired outcome.

8 To add tassels, cut two 8-inch (20-cm) pieces of roving yarn and fold them in half.

Cut a 4-inch (10-cm) piece of embroidery floss and wrap the floss twice around the folded end of the roving, about 1 inch (2.5 cm) from the end. Tie in a knot to secure the tassel and cut off excess floss with scissors.

9 Thread a needle with another 4-inch (10-cm) piece of floss. Stick the needle with floss through the loop on the folded end of the roving tassel and then through a corner of the pillowcase. (PHOTO C)

10 Remove the needle and tie the floss in a tight knot to secure the tassel to the corner of the pillow; use scissors to trim off any excess floss.

11 Repeat the process, making and attaching tassels to all desired corners of the pillows. (PHOTO D)

TIP: Gloves are best when working with dye, but if you like to live on the edge and go without, here are some tried and true concoctions for removing dye from skin:

- Sugar + hand lotion or a body scrub to exfoliate

- Baking soda + warm water as a scrub

- Rubbing alcohol if things are getting serious

- Comet or other strong cleanser scrubbed on skin with a brush as a last resort, followed by soap and water to rinse it away.

MAKER SPOTLIGHT: JUSTINE SILVA

When I was in college, I majored in illustration because I love to draw, but I quickly realized that traditional pen and ink on paper was not enough for me. I took an experimental art class, which opened my eyes to all sorts of different materials as a means of art making. After getting my hands dirty in a laundry list of media, I found my first dream job as a display artist for Anthropologie.

As a retail designer, I have a long history of pulling together "wow moments" of display using unexpected materials on short deadlines with a tight budget. In other words, I am no stranger to collecting soda cans, pulling over at any roadside scrap pile, or scavenging empty wine bottles at bars in the Back Bay of Boston. Sometimes constraints can feel limiting, but there is something special about the ability to see potential and beauty in materials that might otherwise seem ordinary or mundane.

My favorite project while I was on *Making It* was the Shed Hack. I love interior design and have always loved the concept of allowing a space to tell a story of the person that inhabits it. I believe with DIY, art making and styling, there are endless possibilities to transform your space and put your own stamp on it. The size of the shed was daunting at first, but as I got into it, I couldn't help but go a little crazy with bringing the layers of my vision to life. I would love to do this project again—in my own backyard, but maybe with a few more hours of work time.

One of the most important things that I took from my experience on the show was how to manage my self-doubt. Finding direction can be a difficult process, and it's easy to let doubt get in the way of your creativity. Being in a timed environment taught me how to overcome that in a big way—and quick! It's amazing how much you can accomplish when there is quite literally NO TIME for that tiny voice in your head telling you your idea isn't good enough. If you push yourself to follow through and stay true to yourself and your vision, you will be amazed at what you can pull off.

TOTE BAG
WITH A TWIST

You can never have too many tote bags, and this unique dyeing method, similar to a shibori binding technique, makes this new tote to *dye* for! The bloom-like patterns are made by tying string around the twisted canvas of the bag, resulting in beautiful negative space. Plus, it's so easy to whip up a little DIY tassel to add some extra flare. Your grocery store runs have never looked so cool.

SUPPLIES

Plain canvas tote bag

String or baker's twine

Scissors

Fabric dye in desired color (pink or green)

Bucket

Rubber or latex gloves

Cardboard

Yarn in yellow and green

Wooden beads

1. **TO DYE THE TOTE BAG:** Pinch some of the tote bag canvas between your fingers and twist it into a point. Beginning at the base of the point, wrap string tightly around the point, covering the point completely. (PHOTO A)

2. Cut the string and tie a tight knot to secure.

3. Repeat the process of wrapping points of the canvas with string until the desired amount of points is achieved. (Each point will create a blossom of negative space.)

4. Prepare the dye in the bucket according to the package directions. (PHOTO B)

5. While wearing gloves, completely submerge the tote bag in the dye. Let the bag soak according to the package directions. Rinse the bag until water runs clear to remove excess dye.

6. Using scissors, cut the pieces of string and remove.

7. Hang the bag to dry, placing a garbage bag or old towel underneath to catch any drips. For faster drying, hang it outside.

1. **TO MAKE THE TASSEL:** Cut a rectangle of cardboard to the desired tassel length.

2. Wrap the tassel yarn lengthwise around the cardboard until the desired density for the tassel is achieved. (PHOTO C)

3. Cut a 6-inch (15-cm) piece of yarn and string the yarn through one end of the tassel, between the yarn and the cardboard, and then tie the piece of yarn in a tight knot on top.

4. Using scissors, cut through the yarn bundle on the end opposite the knot to remove the tassel from the cardboard.

5. Cut a 10-inch (25-cm) piece of contrasting yarn and wrap the yarn around the tassel two to three times, about 1½ inches (4 cm) from the top. Tie a knot to secure the piece of yarn and cut off the excess using scissors. (PHOTO D) String the beads on the yarn at the top of the tassel.

6. Using scissors, trim the bottom of the tassel to create even ends.

7. Tie the tassel to the tote bag handle.

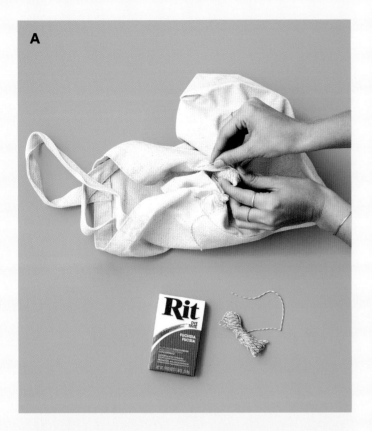

A

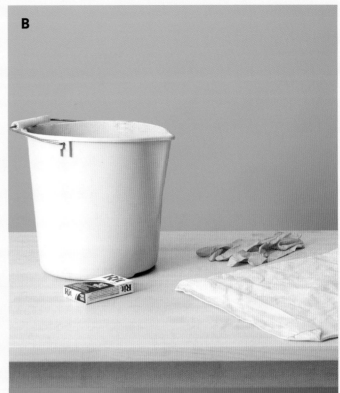

B

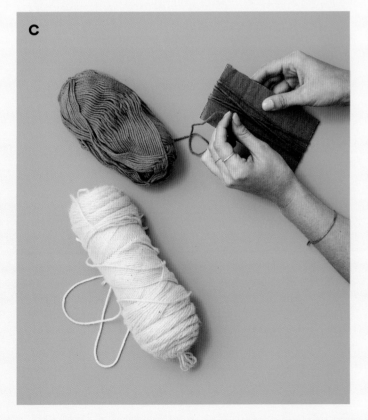

C

D

DREAM-HOME
PIGGY BANK

No offense to the piggy-shaped banks we all used in our younger days—but grown-ups can use an inspiring place to save, too! Makers were tasked to make piggy banks that represented their savings end goal, and the results weren't only inspiring, they made a lot of *cents*.

SUPPLIES

Drill with ³⁄₁₆-inch (5-mm) and ½-inch (12-mm) bits

Wood shadow-box house

Thin plexiglass sheet

Sharpie

Glass cutter (plexiglass can also be cut at most home-improvement stores)

Decorative paper

Pencil

Scissors

Multi-surface acrylic paint (choose an accent color)

Paintbrush

Foam brush

Mod Podge

Hot glue gun filled with glue

Decorative items (such as a dollhouse door, sconce, faux plants, doormat, etc.)

Painter's tape

Screwdriver

Mini gold screws

1 Using the drill with a ½-inch (12-mm) bit, drill several holes in a row to create an open slot for money in the roof of the shadow-box house.

2 Place the house, open side down, on top of the plexiglass sheet. Trace with a Sharpie and set the shadow box aside.

3 Using a glass cutter, cut along the traced line on the plexiglass sheet. Or, take the sheet to a home-improvement store for cutting. Set aside.

4 Place the house, open side down, on decorative paper and trace it with a pencil. Cut out the house shape using scissors. (PHOTO A)

5 Paint the front edge of the house with an accent color using the paintbrush. Apply two coats and let the paint dry completely. (PHOTO B)

6 Using a foam brush, apply a layer of Mod Podge to the back interior wall of the house and the back side of the decorative paper house cutout.

7 Place the decorative paper on the back wall of the house, Mod Podge side down. Smooth the paper gently with your fingers to remove any bubbles and adhere the paper to the wall. Let dry for 15–20 minutes.

8 With the foam brush, apply a thin layer of Mod Podge on top of the decorative paper to seal. Let dry completely.

9 Add desired decorative elements and use hot glue to secure the items.

10 Place the house-shaped plexiglass sheet on top of the open side of the shadow box and secure the sheet with tape to eliminate movement. Using a ³⁄₁₆-inch (5-mm) bit, drill holes through the sheet and into the house on the four square corners of the house.

11 Using a screwdriver, attach the screws. (PHOTO C) Remove and discard the tape.

12 Insert money through the slot in the roof. When you're ready to buy your dream house, remove the screws and plexiglass, grab your loot, then reattach. (PHOTO D)

HEXAGON
WALL SHELVES

SHED HACK!

This project is not exactly for the seasoned woodworker, but instead can be made by a Maker who may not know a miter from a circular saw and is more than fine with that. These hexagon shelves will add some cool, geometric dimension to your space and will let you whet your woodworking appetite without needing to know what a rasp tool does. Inspired by the Shed Hack challenge on the show, these shelves added some great personality to a tiny space—and they can do the same for you!

SUPPLIES

Three 4- or 6-inch by 6-foot (10- or 15-cm by 1.8-m) pieces of wood (about 1 inch/2.5 cm thick)

Miter saw

Peel and stick wallpaper

Scissors

Pencil

Wood glue

Staple gun

Sandpaper

Sponge brush

Multi-surface acrylic paint in three colors

Wood stain and brush (if applicable)

Hammer

Nails or brackets

1. If cutting the wood yourself, set the miter saw to 30 degrees and cut six 8-inch (20-cm) pieces of wood, making sure that the cuts on both ends of each piece are angled inward.

2. Lay out the wallpaper, backing side up. Place the cut wood pieces on the wallpaper and trace with a pencil.

3. Cut out the wallpaper along the traced lines using scissors.

4. Peel off the backing and apply the wallpaper to the interior side of the wood pieces. (PHOTO A)

5. Create the hexagon by applying wood glue to all of the joints, then pressing them together. Let dry for an hour. (PHOTO B)

6. Flip over the hexagon and staple each joint together with two staples. Let dry for 24 hours.

7. Once the hexagon is dry, sand any uneven corners.

8. Repeat steps 1–7 to make three shelves in all.

9. Paint or stain the outside of the shelves as desired. Let dry. (PHOTO C)

10. To hang the shelves, hammer nails into the wall so they will be disguised in the top corners of each hexagon, or use a bracket to hang each shelf.

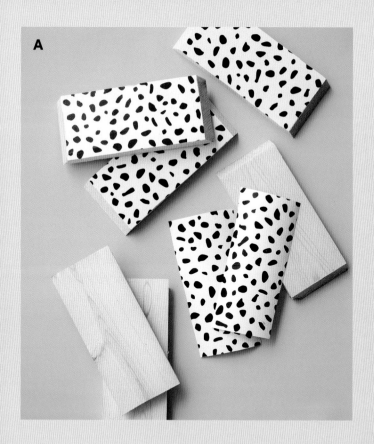

TIP: When painting the accent on your shelves, keep some sandpaper or a paint scraper nearby. If you slip up and get paint on an area of the wood you were hoping to keep bare, let it dry completely and then sand or scrape it off.

YOU ARE
WHAT YOU EAT

Have you ever thought about what food best represents you? We've got the perfect recipe for making felt into a pizza, a taco, a cheeseburger, ice cream, and ice pops that look good enough to eat—and they might also be a great representation of your innermost self. Even better? They make the perfect partner for the Food Truck on page 137. (And don't worry—while this project may look like you'll have to whip up a felt feast, you'll soon find yourself with the best kind of fast food!)

Assorted 9 x 12-inch
(23 x 30.5-cm) craft felt
sheets (2 tan, 2 cream,
2 red, 1 green, 1 black,
1 dark red, 1 gray)

Pizza pattern pieces
(see page 186)

Scissors

Embroidery floss
(tan, green, dark red,
light pink)

Embroidery needle

Cotton batting

FELT PIZZA

1 Cut the felt using the templates and color suggestions in the photos.

2 **FOR THE CRUST:** Lay one pizza crust piece on top of another and blanket stitch around the outside (curved) edge with tan floss.

3 Stuff batting against the stitched edge, creating a raised crust along the edge. Stitch along the inside of the crust edge, about ¾ inch (2 cm) from the edge, using a running stitch to keep the batting in place.

4 Blanket stitch the straight edges together.

5 Repeat steps 2–4 to create four finished crust pieces.

6 **FOR THE TOPPINGS:**
Pepperoni: Blanket stitch two circles together using matching floss, hiding the thread ends on the inside.

Green pepper: Sew two ends of two green strips together with green floss. Take a third strip and sew it to the ends of the other two strips. Turn the circle so the ends point in, forming a green pepper ring.

7 **TO ASSEMBLE THE PIZZA:** Place the red sauce quarters on top of the crust, followed by the cheese quarters and desired toppings.

8 Attach the pieces with glue, if desired, or keep loose for continuous play.

Assorted 9 x 12-inch
(23 x 30.5-cm) craft
felt sheets (2 yellow,
1 green, 1 red, 1 brown,
1 yellow-orange)

Taco pattern pieces
(see page 186)

Scissors

2 yellow pipe cleaners

Cotton batting

Embroidery floss
(yellow, red, brown)

Embroidery needle

FELT TACO

1 Cut the felt following the pattern.

2 **FOR THE TACO SHELL:** Twist the ends of two pipe cleaners together to create one long pipe cleaner.

3 Arrange the pipe cleaners around the outer edge of one of the shell pieces and twist the pipe cleaner ends together to make a circle to fit. Lay the other shell piece on top.

4 Blanket stitch the shell pieces together with yellow floss, wrapping the stitches around the pipe cleaner.

5 **FOR THE BEEF:** Fold the beef piece in half.

6 Stuff with batting.

7 Blanket stitch the open edge with brown floss.

8 **FOR THE TOMATOES:** Stitch the desired tomato segments on each tomato piece to give the look of slices with orange floss using a running stitch.

9 Fold the tomato pieces in half.

10 Sew along the open edges with orange floss using a running stitch.

11 **TO ASSEMBLE THE TACO:** Fold the taco shell in half and layer the beef, cheese, lettuce, and tomatoes inside.

12 Attach the pieces to the taco with glue, if desired, or keep loose for continuous play.

Assorted 9 x 12-inch
(23 x 30.5-cm) craft felt
sheets (1 tan, 1 cream,
1 brown, 1 red, 1 yellow-
orange, 1 green)

Cheeseburger pattern
pieces (see page 187)

Scissors

Embroidery floss
(cream, brown, orange)

Embroidery needle

Cotton batting

FELT CHEESEBURGER

1. Cut the felt following the pattern.

2. **FOR THE BUN:** On one of the outside bun pieces, sew scattered French knots with cream floss to look like sesame seeds.

3. Blanket stitch the sesame-topped outside piece and an inside piece together with cream floss, stopping halfway around to stuff with batting.

4. Finish stitching around the top bun.

5. Blanket stitch the remaining outside and inside bun pieces together with cream floss, stopping halfway around to stuff with batting.

6. Finish stitching around the bottom bun.

7. **FOR THE BURGER:** Blanket stitch the burger pieces together with brown floss, stopping halfway around to stuff with batting.

8. Finish stitching the burger.

9. **FOR THE TOMATO:** Back stitch the tomato pieces together along the edge (about ¼ inch [6 mm] from the edge) with orange floss.

10. **FOR THE TOMATOES:** Stitch the desired tomato segments on each tomato piece to give the look of slices with orange floss using a running stitch.

11. **TO ASSEMBLE THE CHEESE-BURGER:** Place the burger on top of the bottom bun, followed by the cheese, tomato, and lettuce. Top with seeded bun.

12. Attach the pieces with glue, if desired, or keep loose for continuous play.

Assorted 9 x 12-inch (23 x 30.5-cm) craft felt sheets (1 tan, 1 white, 1 mint)

Ice cream pattern pieces (see page 187)

Scissors

Embroidery floss (cream, brown, orange, other colors for sprinkles)

Embroidery needle

Foam ball

Cardboard cone

Hot glue gun filled with glue

FELT ICE CREAM

1 Cut the felt following the pattern to make two ice cream cones.

2 Use straight stitches or French knots in desired color(s) to create sprinkles on the ice cream pieces.

3 Stitch around the edge of the ice cream pieces with a loose running stitch and corresponding floss color. Don't tie off the floss.

4 Place a foam ball inside each of the ice cream pieces and pull the floss to cinch the felt around the ball.

5 Pull tight and tie off the floss. Set aside.

6 Fold the ruffle piece in half lengthwise.

7 Stitch a loose running stitch in the corresponding floss color down the length of the ruffle. Don't tie off the floss.

8 Pull the floss so the felt creates a ruffle.

9 Measure the ruffle to match the bottom of the ice cream ball and connect the two ends with a few stitches around the ball.

10 Use hot glue to cover the cardboard cone with the felt cone piece.

11 Use hot glue to attach each ice cream ball and ruffle to each cone.

Assorted 9 x 12-inch
(23 x 30.5-cm) craft felt
sheets (1 blue, 1 pink,
1 white, 1 brown, other
colors for sprinkles)

Ice pops pattern pieces
(see page 187)

Scissors

Embroidery floss (teal,
hot pink, white, brown,
other colors for sprinkles)

Embroidery needle

Ice pop sticks

Hot glue gun filled
with glue

Cotton batting,
or foam cut to shape

FELT ICE POPS

1. Cut the felt following the pattern to make two ice pops.

2. Backstitch the top or bottom drip pieces on the ice pop pieces, matching the colors shown in the photo on page 98 (i.e., top drip on pink pop, bottom drip on blue pop).

3. Use straight stitches in desired colors to embellish the ice pop pieces with sprinkles.

4. Blanket stitch the ice pop pieces together with a corresponding floss color, leaving the bottom open.

5. Stuff the ice pops with cotton batting or the foam shape.

6. Hot glue an ice pop stick inside the open end of each pop.

7. Finish the blanket stitch on the bottom of the ice pops to close.

TIP: If you'd like to keep your stitches invisible and avoid having to change embroidery floss colors too often, opt for stitching with fishing line or monofilament. You can still add in a pop of color and texture by attaching beads for your ice cream sprinkles and sesame seed bun!

PAINTED TILE ART

Although the use of tile is central in DIY home-improvement projects, it's an underutilized surface in crafting. This is probably because it is associated more frequently with the floor in the bathroom than the art over the bookcase. However, when a Maker used herringbone tiles to beautifully brighten walls in the Shed Hack Challenge, we got the idea to turn tiles into framed art to make a bold statement in the home.

SUPPLIES

Painted tile pattern (see page 189)

Pencil

Four 12-inch (30.5-cm) square white tile sheets with repeating hexagon pattern

Multi-surface acrylic paint in desired colors

Small paintbrush

Spray sealant

2-foot (60-cm) square canvas

Hot glue gun filled with glue

Picture frame (optional)

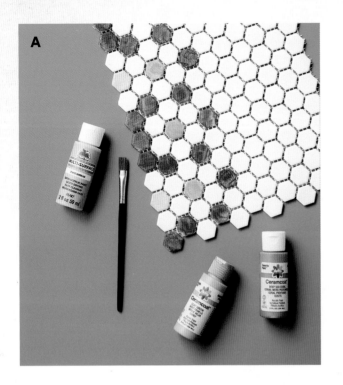

A

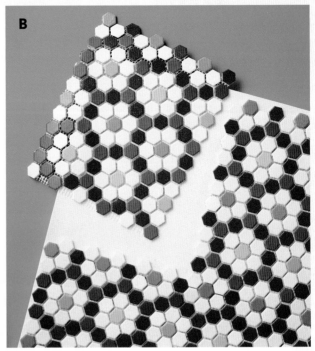

B

1 If desired, use the template as a map and mark the tiles with a pencil to designate which color to paint each tile (e.g., "R" for red tiles, "Y" for yellow).

Paint the tiles according to the pattern with a small paintbrush. Wash brushes thoroughly between paint color changes. Apply several coats to cover the tiles thoroughly, letting them dry completely between each coat. (PHOTO A)

2 Spray the tiles with a sealant to give them shine and protect them from scratches. Attach the sheets of tiles to the canvas, octagons interlocking, using a generous amount of hot glue. (PHOTO B)

3 Frame, if desired, and display.

TIP: If you can only find a sheet of hexagon tiles in colors other than white, spray the sheet with a couple of coats of white spray paint to give you a fresh pallette to start from. A white surface makes acrylic paint colors pop! You can also select tiles in any shape—square, rectangle, subway pattern—and create a design of your own!

MAKER SPOTLIGHT: JO GICK

I spend most of my days working with clients and helping them realize their dream homes. I love my job, but have always spent my spare time making—for me, my friends, and even for my clients. Making has always been an escape for me. I love getting lost in my latest project and the problem solving that's needed, as well as the satisfaction of making something with my hands.

As I'm an interior designer by trade, the Shed Hack challenge on the show was made for me. I felt the most at home creating in this way. I knew that I needed great focal points and a feeling of cohesiveness in my space, and I decided to make my shed a Maker space. It is tough to always be inspired, and I believe the spaces you surround yourself with can really spark creativity.

Not only do I love color—the herringbone back wall of my shed can attest to that—but I also love pattern. I am attracted to geometric shapes and wanted to make sure those were present in my shed as well. This is where the floor came into play. I took some natural wood hexagons and painted them to create an interesting pattern on the floor. I wanted to preserve the natural wood, but still add a bit of color and gold accent to make it just a bit more interesting. I really felt this space was cohesive, happy, and unqiue to me, and I even have a patch to prove it!

Another favorite was creating the children's fort. A rainbow came to mind first, but I really wanted to make it soft and safe for children—I have two children of my own and know how important it is that the fort would be something safe for them. Then I thought of pool noodles. I knew that if I bent them in a half circle I was halfway there to a great rainbow. The sunshine sign and cute cloud pillows were icing on the cake to a very happy place to be.

UNCONVENTIONAL DOOR WREATH

Wreaths can be a staple for any occasion or holiday, so why not make a statement with your front door décor? Unconventional materials can say even more than your garden-variety wreath—so we turned to a bike wheel to help welcome guests. We love the juxtaposition of the delicate paper flowers and industrial metal, and we think you're *wheelie* gonna love it.

SUPPLIES

Bike wheel

Spray paint

Clear sealant (optional)

Flower pattern pieces (see pages 184-185)

Pencil

Cardstock in various colors (light pink, dark pink, coral, cream, light yellow, yellow, gold, orange, light green, dark green)

Scissors

Hot glue gun filled with glue

Floral wire ribbon

1 Spray-paint the bike wheel with two coats of paint and let dry completely between each coat. If hanging the wreath outside, spray with a clear sealant and let dry.

2 Using the templates and a pencil, trace the flower pieces onto the cardstock according to the colors shown in the photo.

3 Using scissors or a craft cutter, cut out the flower pieces. (PHOTO A)

4 MAKE FIVE OF FLOWER 2: Working from the tip of the petal and moving to the center, gently roll the flower petals for Flower 2 around a pencil to curl them up and add dimension. Place a dot of hot glue in the center of the largest flower piece (2-A) and place the next largest flower piece on top (2-B). Repeat the process with the remaining flower pieces and contrasting centers (orange in the center of the gold flower, cream in the center of the coral flower), stacking them from largest to smallest (2-C through G).

5 MAKE TWO OF FLOWER 4: Gently fold the petals of Flower

C

triangle pieces at the bottom of the cup so they face outward. Fold each of the arms of the 5-D pieces so they point up. (This will create the eye of the daffodil.) Place a dot of hot glue in the center of the 5-A piece and press the 5-B piece into it. Place a dot of hot glue on each of the 5-C pieces on the bottom of the cup piece and press it into the center of the stacked 5-A and 5-B pieces. Place another dot of glue in the middle of the cup and press a 5-D piece in the center. Repeat to make the other daffodils.

4-A in half lengthwise to create dimension. Pinch the ends of Flower 4-B together to make them stand up. Place a dot of hot glue in the center of Flower 4-A and place Flower 4-B on top. Repeat until all Flower 4 pieces are stacked and glued together.

6 MAKE FOUR OF FLOWER 5: Gently fold the Flower 5-A petals around a pencil, lengthwise, to add dimension. Fold each 5-C piece into a cylinder and secure the cylinder with a dot of hot glue. (PHOTO B) (This will create the cup or corona of the daffodil.) Fold the

7 MAKE EIGHT BRANCHES OF GREENERY: Gently fold the leaves of the branches around a pencil lengthwise. Cut a piece of floral wire to the length of the stem. Attach the stem to the wire using hot glue.

8 Once all the flowers and leaves are assembled, begin by attaching the largest flowers to the bike wheel using hot glue. (PHOTO C) Once the largest flowers are secure, fill in open spaces with smaller flowers and the greenery using hot glue.

9 Loop a ribbon through the wreath and hang the ribbon on a door or wall.

MASTER CRAFTS

ANIMAL INSTINCTS

We all have an animal that best represents our most inner selves. Maybe it's a dog or a horse or a turtle or a bat or maybe . . . it's a unicorn! For the unicorn inside each of us, here's a rather lovely one that's easy to sew, easy to put up, and easy to customize so that it's undeniably you.

SUPPLIES

Unicorn sewing patterns (see page 183)

½ yard white felt

9 x 12-inch (23 x 30.5-cm) light pink craft felt sheet

8 inches (20 cm) faux leather, gold

Poly-fil or other synthetic fiberfill

1 skein (5 oz., 280 yds) multicolored yarn

Scissors

Pen or fabric marker

Pins

Sewing needle and thread

Sewing machine

Tape

Turning tool

Crown embellishments (beads, felt scraps, pom-poms)

Wooden plaque

Acrylic paint in desired color for plaque

Paintbrush

Hot glue gun filled with glue

1. Print and cut all pattern pieces. (PHOTO A)

2. Trace and cut all felt pieces according to pattern (¼ inch [6 mm] seam allowances are included).

3. Fold the fabric for the horn. Place and trace the horn on the fold as indicated on the pattern. Do not cut.

4. Sew the horn on the mark from "A" to "B."

5. Cut out the horn, cutting close to the seam (about ¹⁄₁₆ inch [2 mm] away).

6. Sew the body from "A" to "B" and from "C" to "D." Backstitch to secure the seam on the top of the head.

7. Fold the nose, aligning the edges. Sew at ¼ inch (6 mm).

8. Glue the pink part of the ears to the ear pieces with hot glue. When dry, fold the bottom sides toward the center and pin in place. (PHOTO B)

9. Cut right on the mark at the top of the head and open it. Align the seams together and pin in place. Put the ears inside one of the open seams on each side, folded toward the nose side. Pin in place.

10. Sew the opening to close it. Be careful to catch the ears in the seam and to close the whole opening. (PHOTO C) Turn and fill the body with Poly-fil.

11. Trace and cut the piece "back." Baste all around the "fabric back" piece.

12. Pull the thread to close the fabric. Tighten the fabric and secure the seam with a knot.

13. Place piece on the back of the body. Sew all around to enclose the stuffing.

14. Pinch both sides of the nose to form nostrils. Sew in place.

15. Turn the horn using a turning tool. Stuff the horn using just a bit of Poly-fil in the tip.

16. Baste around the base of the horn at about a quarter of an inch. Pull the thread to close the opening. (PHOTO D)

17. Starting at the base of the horn, wrap thread around the horn to the top in a spiral. Insert needle

CONTINUED ➡

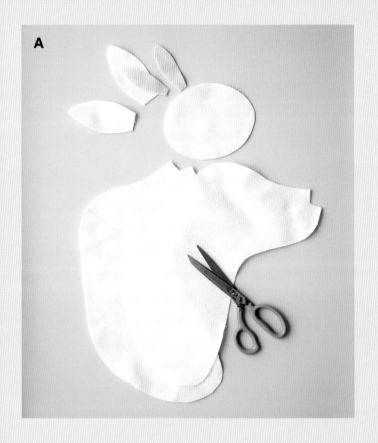

A

B

C

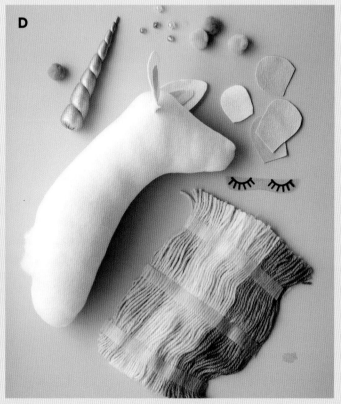

D

at the back tip of the horn and make a knot. Cut the thread as close to the fabric as possible.

18 Place the horn on top of the head. Sew all around.

19 To make the mane, tape the beginning end of the yarn on one corner of the cardboard. Wrap the yarn horizontally around the cardboard (width-wise) until the cardboard is covered with yarn, leaving about an inch on the top and bottom of the cardboard.

20 Cut the yarn and tape the end to the cardboard.

21 Apply one piece of tape to the yarn vertically along each edge of the cardboard (so four strips in total). Make sure the tape adheres to all the yarn pieces, but not the cardboard. This is to hold the yarn in place once you remove the cardboard.

22 Apply tape down the center of one side of the yarn, do not tape the cardboard, and do not cut the tape.

23 Slide the cardboard out from the yarn. Keep the ends of the yarn aligned, using the tape as a guide.

Carefully turn over and continue the center tape on this side, making sure not to bunch up the yarn but to keep the strands flat. Tape any additional areas to create a secure piece before sewing.

24 Sew 2 to 3 passes with a sewing machine along the tape at the center of the yarn piece. Cut along the sides where the yarn was wrapped to create fringe. Fold in at the seam to test that all yarn strands are secure; sew another pass if any were missed. Remove all tape once sewn completely. You now have a sewn seam down the middle of the yarn, with fringe on both sides.

25 Place the mane on the head, starting at the base of the horn. Align the mane seam with the seam on the unicorn back. Sew the mane on the unicorn with the needle and thread.

26 Trim the mane as desired. Create a crown by applying beads, pom-poms, and felt shapes around the horn using hot glue.

27 Paint the plaque. Apply two coats and let dry completely. Mount the unicorn to the plaque using hot glue.

MAKER SPOTLIGHT: AMBER KEMP-GERSTEL

I'm a child of the '80s. The era of puffy stickers, embellished denim jackets, friendship bracelets, and neon everything. It's hard to imagine how any child of the '80s *didn't* grow up to become a professional Maker.

Despite my birth year, my path to full-time blogger, crafter, and television DIY expert was pretty circuitous. I first explored the world of being a child psychologist . . . complete with four years in grad school, one year for a dissertation, and two years in clinical training. When I launched my blog, *Damask Love*, it was initially a side hustle, but within a few years, it grew into much more. Turns out the path led me to six weeks on set with the likes of Amy Poehler and Nick Offerman to film the first show of its type . . . crafting and prime time and me? Yes, girl, it was happening.

My approach to the entire *Making It* process was to bring my absolute best but stay 100 percent true to my style and voice. That unicorn head? It didn't win a patch but let me tell you this: I would hang that girl in my craft room any day of the week! My circus tent play fort? We literally have a version of this in our home! Everything I create is colorful, doable, and has a hefty dose of quirk (a word that Simon regularly used to describe my projects!).

Perhaps my most doable project was the rope-wrapped bucket stools! Even Amy admitted she could give them a try. Who knew that a plastic bucket, some rope, and a hot glue gun could result in something so "chic" (Simon's word, not mine). Slightly more ambitious was the unicorn head . . . it took *forever* to create the pattern, but with that done, it came together quickly during the first Faster Craft challenge.

I couldn't be prouder of my time in the *Making It* barn. I made awesome crafts and even better memories. Best memory: Amy Poehler swiped a pair of scissors from set. Scandalous! You heard it here first.

BEADED RESIN LETTERS

Crafting is all about testing out new methods that can elevate the ordinary, and working with resin does just that! Resin is a crafting medium that can take some practice to master, but once you get the hang of it, it's sure to start a new obsession. Resin can be used to embed or encase almost anything in crystal-clear plastic, so as to better display some prized treasures, like these colorful beads. Just mix, pour, and you (and your beads) will be set!

SUPPLIES

Utility knife

Chipboard letters

White acrylic paint

Paintbrush

Mod Podge

Paintbrush

Plastic drop cloth

Pourable resin (three letters uses about 2 quarts/2 L of mixed resin, i.e., 1 quart/1 L each of clear epoxy resin and clear epoxy hardener)

Rubber gloves

2 disposable containers

2 wooden paint stirrers

Cardboard box large enough to cover the letters

Assorted beads

Hot glue gun filled with glue

Drinking straw

1. Using a utility knife, remove the front panel of the chipboard letters and any interior pieces to create hollow chipboard letters. (PHOTO A)

2. Paint the letters with two to three coats of white paint. Let the paint dry completely between each coat.

3. Apply a generous layer of Mod Podge to each letter using a paint-brush. Let the Mod Podge dry completely. (PHOTO B)

4. Before mixing the resin, cover an even work surface with a garbage bag or plastic drop cloth, and put on your gloves. Prepare half of the total required resin according to the package directions. Generally this means mixing an equal amount of clear epoxy resin and clear epoxy hardener (16 ounces/480 ml of each if you're making three letters in all) in a disposable container with a wooden paint stirrer or large wooden craft stick, then mixing it slowly (to help avoid bubbles) for about 5 minutes.

5. Fill each letter halfway with resin. If desired, cover the letters with a cardboard box to prevent dust or debris from landing in the resin. Let the resin cure completely according to package directions. (PHOTO C) Dispose of the used mixing tools. Do not reuse for the next batch of resin.

6. Once the resin is cured completely, glue the beads directly onto the resin using a hot glue gun. (PHOTO D)

7. Prepare the remaining resin (1 quart/1 L total for three letters) as described in step 4 and slowly pour it over the beads until the resin just fills the letters. Do not overfill.

   If bubbles are present, hover over the bubbles with a straw and gently blow through the straw to remove them.

8. Cover with the box and let the resin cure completely before displaying the letters.

~~~~~~~~~~~~~~~~~~~~~~~~~~~~~~

TIP: Remove resin from skin (preferably before it cures) by soaking a paper towel or cloth with vinegar and rubbing until the resin begins to peel. If that doesn't work, try acetone or acetone nail polish remover in a well-ventilated area, and that should do the trick.

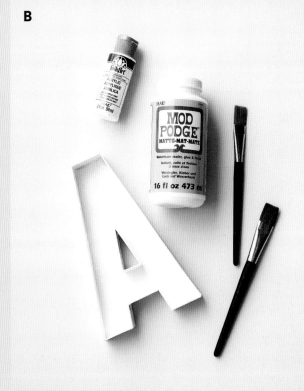

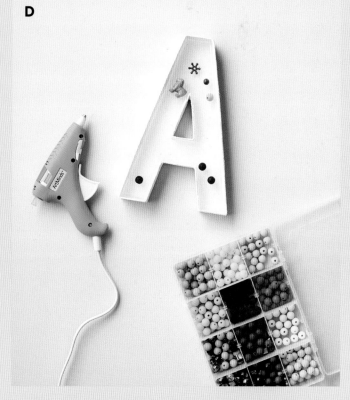

RAINBOW PLAY TENT

Dorothy sang about all of the good stuff you can find over the rainbow, but we think the real magic happens under it! This genius rainbow play tent was designed by an incredible Maker for kids and is constructed out of pool noodles wrapped in felt, creating the perfect spot for reading and daydreaming, where troubles melt like lemon drops.

SUPPLIES

FOR THE PLAY TENT:

Twenty-one 52-inch (1.3-m) foam pool noodles

Duct tape

Seven 12 by 80-inch (30.5-cm by 2-m) pieces of felt in various colors

Hot glue gun filled with glue

Scissors

1 yard (about 90 cm) white felt

Two 36-inch (90-cm) pieces of wooden molding

Staple gun

Yarn or string

FOR THE CLOUD PILLOW:

2 yards (about 1.8 m) white felt

Scissors

Sewing machine

Assorted 9 x 12-inch (23 x 30.5-cm) craft felt sheets (1 black, 1 peach)

Hot glue gun filled with glue

Poly-fil or other synthetic fiberfill

Needle

White thread

FOR THE PLAY TENT:

1 Using scissors, cut 7 noodles in half.

2 Connect a half-noodle piece to a full noodle by wrapping the ends together several times with duct tape. Repeat until you have 14 extended noodles that are each 1½ noodles long. (PHOTO A)

3 Tape two of these noodles together, side by side, by wrapping them in duct tape on either end and at the junction where the two noodles are connected. Repeat the process until you have created seven sets of noodles total. (PHOTO B)

4 Lay out one color of felt on a flat surface. Place one set of taped noodles on the felt and secure the felt to the noodles with hot glue on one side.

5 Once the felt is secure on one side of the noodles (glueing the sides will help to hide any glued areas when the full tent is assembled), tightly wrap the noodles twice in the felt. Secure the felt with a generous amount of hot glue to seal. (PHOTO C)

6 Cut off excess felt, leaving about 2 inches (5 cm) of felt on each end of the noodles.

7 Continue this process with different colors of felt until you have seven sets of noodles wrapped in various colors.

8 Lay out the white felt to form the base of the tent. This piece will keep the tent together once the noodles are attached.

9 Place a piece of molding on each of the short ends of the fabric. While holding the end of the fabric and the molding, roll the molding toward the fabric once to cover it with felt.

10 Attach the felt to the moldings using staples. (PHOTO D)

11 Once the felt is attached to the moldings, roll the molding pieces toward the center, twice, to cover. Lift the inside edge of the molding and place a line of hot glue underneath it to secure. Press molding back into felt and glue and let set.

12 Fold the felt on each end of the moldings underneath itself

CONTINUED ➡

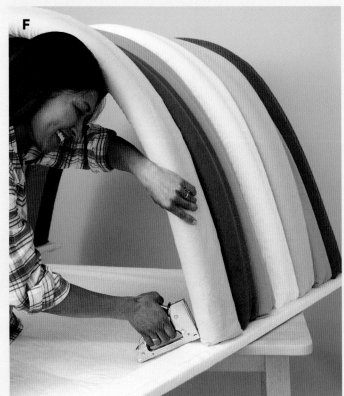

(the way you might fold wrapping paper around the end of a box) and secure to the molding with staples.

13 Beginning at one end of the molding and working toward the other end, attach the felt-wrapped noodles to the top of a piece of molding by stapling the 2 inches (5 cm) of felt on each end of the noodles to the molding, getting as close to the noodles as possible to secure them in place. Tuck any excess fabric under the noodles to hide. (PHOTO E)

14 Repeat the process with the other piece of molding and the opposite ends of the noodles until all of the noodles are stapled to both pieces of molding. (PHOTO F)

15 Tie the tops of the noodles together using a piece of yarn or string. This will hold them close together while you secure them with glue. Put a few large dots of hot glue between the noodles at the top of the rainbow to glue them to one another.

16 Once the glue is set, cut and remove the yarn.

FOR THE CLOUD PILLOW:

1 Cut the white felt into a cloud shape. (PHOTO G)

2 Using a sewing machine, sew around the edge with a ¼-inch (6-mm) seam allowance, leaving a 3-inch (7.5-cm) opening at the bottom for stuffing.

3 Turn the pillow right side out.

4 Cut the craft felt into face-shaped pieces. Use black for two eyes and the smile, and peach for the rosy cheeks.

5 Apply the face pieces to the pillow using hot glue.

6 Stuff the pillow with Poly-fil. (PHOTO H)

7 Close the opening at the base of the pillow by hand-sewing with an invisible stitch.

FOOD TRUCK

It may seem like child's play, but we have to *taco*-bout how awesome this food truck is! Our version here is made out of cardboard and is perfect for pairing with our felt food (see page 99). This simple food truck design can be decorated to serve whatever culinary creations your kiddos come up with, no reservations required.

SUPPLIES

4 corrugated cardboard display boards (3 by 4 feet each)

Utility knife

Spray paint (silver and black for wheels; color of choice for body of truck, optional)

4 large paper plates

4 small paper plates

Hot glue gun filled with glue

Acrylic craft paint (in various colors)

Paintbrushes

1. Take two of the display boards and, using a utility knife, cut off the side pieces at the pre-made folds. This will give you two large pieces and four smaller pieces. Set aside.

2. Following the template on page 188, cut the sides of the food truck from the remaining two display boards (using one full board for each), along with their corresponding slits and tabs (as indicated on the template) for added security when assembling. **(PHOTO A)**

3. Cut the top and windshield from the two reserved large pieces, along with their corresponding tabs and slits, according to the template.

4. Cut the hood, grill, and shelf from the four reserved small pieces, along with their designated tabs and slits, according to the template.

5. If desired, spray paint the truck pieces in the color of your choice. Let dry.

6. Spray paint the large paper plates black and the small paper plates silver. Let dry.

7. Put the silver paper plates (the hubcaps), bottom sides up, on top of the black plates (the tires), right sides up. Glue the hubcaps to the wheels with hot glue to make the wheels. **(PHOTO B)**

8. Attach the wheels to the sides of the truck with hot glue (the wheels should touch the floor).

9. Paint and decorate the exterior of the truck with acrylic paint as desired. **(PHOTO C)**

CONTINUED ➡

10 Assemble the food truck. With a partner or using a wall to help stablize each the side pieces, attach the roof to the sides by sliding the side tabs into the corresponding roof slits. (Depending on the weight of the cardboard used, you may have to enlarge the slits a bit during assembly. Keep a utility knife nearby to englarge the slits, if necessary.) Attaching the roof first will give the truck enough structure to stand while the rest of the elements are added.

11 Continue assembly by attaching the grill, then the window pieces. Slide each of the tabs into their corresponding slits on the side pieces, using a utility knife to make adustments to the slits where needed. (**PHOTO D**)

12 Once all of the structural pieces of the truck are assembled (sides, roof, grill, window), reinforce the structure by adding a line of hot glue where each tab meets its slit. You can also add a line of hot glue to any other seams of the truck where added stability is desired.

13 Glue the shelf pieces to the inner wall of the truck and to the side window, using hot glue.

14 Add decorative elements to truck (menu, awning, truck name, etc.) with acrylic paint, if desired. Let dry completely.

~~~~~~~~~~~~~~~~~~~~

TIP: Looking for creative ideas for your own perfect food truck? Check out #foodtruck on Instagram! Not only will the food offerings make your stomach growl, but you'll find thousands of cool truck designs that can help inspire your own DIY version.

MAKER SPOTLIGHT: BILLY KHEEL

I'm not sure whether I found felt or felt found me. All my life, I've been passionate about sports and loved the nature of competition and the controlled athleticism. But always hanging around the edges of sports was this soft material—in felt pennants, felt jackets, or felt banners, it seemed there was some felt around. I loved how hard-fought athletic achievements were commemorated in this fuzzy fabric. I started making my own pennants and loved using felt to make out of the ordinary things. I've found that people think of felt as an outdated craft or something for kids' toys and are intrigued to see nineties sports cards and urban rivers in this fabric.

Another surprising thing about felt is that it got me on *Making It*. I guess they thought my weird take on this craft material would give me chance to inspire people to do their own craft projects. For any kind of Maker, this show is a dream come true. We hung out all day in an amazing craft barn with a bunch of other fun people who also liked creating rad projects. Of course, we were all under serious time pressure and judged on everything we did, but it was still tons of laughing and a chance to spend all day being inspired and doing cool challenges with all sorts of materials.

One of the challenges was making a kids' fort with a puzzle to go along with it. I live in Los Angeles and spend about 20 percent of my time eating tacos from food trucks, so my first thought was "Could a taco truck be a fort? Is a taco a puzzle?" I took my inspiration from eighties action movies and called mine "Action Tacos." And making tacos is totally a puzzle: you make the different ingredients separately, and then combine them into your own special taco. After I made my patch-winning taco truck, so many different people and their kids were inspired to make their own taco trucks and their own tacos to go with them. The best part of this project was then seeing people become inspired to come together and make their own trucks that express their imagination.

CROSS-STITCH
WALL ART

〰〰〰〰〰〰〰〰〰〰〰

Think back to a favorite craft from your childhood; whether it was finger painting or ice pop stick art, indulge in the nostalgia that comes with revisiting your earliest days as a maker. For lots of us, cross-stitch was a first foray into making, and this oversized cross-stitch art takes an old favorite to the next level, resulting in a piece of graphic art that is sure to make a big statement in your home, without a stitch of stress.

SUPPLIES

Scissors

Yarn in various weights, in navy, hunter green, mustard, light blue, and teal

Yarn needle

Cross-stitch pattern (see page 182)

Pegboard

Hot glue gun filled with glue

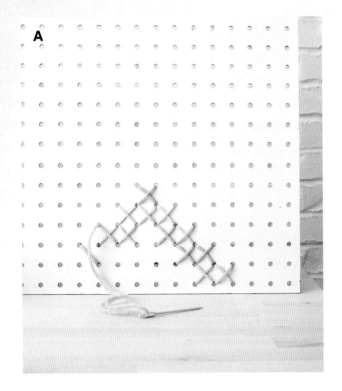

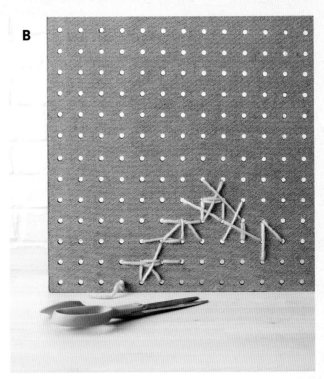

1. Use the cross-stitch pattern on page 182 or map out your own design according to the size of the pegboard you have selected. For instance, if your pegboard has 48 rows of squares horizontally and 24 squares vertically, then you will match that same number of squares on your cross-stitch pattern to determine where to stitch. This may mean doing a simple, small cross stitch pattern with few squares if your pegboard is small, or only doing a portion of a larger pattern, then cropping it to the amount of squares available on the pegboard.

c

2 Cut off a long piece of yarn and thread it through the needle.

3 Following the cross-stitch pattern, stitch an X in the pegboard squares by bringing the threaded needle from the back of the pegboard, through the top left hole of the square, moving horizontally on the top of the pegboard, then through the bottom right hole of the square and out to the back of the pegboard. Next, bring the needle through the top right hole of the same square, crossing over the first stitch, horizontally, and out the bottom left hole, forming an X. (PHOTO A)

4 Work in colored sections, stitching Xs in each square, according to the pattern.

5 Once a section is completed, cut the yarn, leaving a few inches, and tie off the yarn with a big knot on the back of the pegboard, or glue the end of the yarn to the back of the pegboard using hot glue. (PHOTO B)

6 Repeat steps 1–3 until the pattern is completed.

7 Display the finished piece. (PHOTO C)

DIP-DYED MACRAMÉ
WALL HANGING

SHED HACK!

Macramé is a form of fiber art using knots that was popular in the 1970s and has made a big comeback as of late. If you love working with your hands, this still-groovy trend can be used to make everything from clothing to hanging planters, and it can be dyed, beaded, and embellished to suit your taste. This basic macramé wall hanging uses two types of simple knots and is a great project to get you started. We literally can-*knot* wait to see what you make!

SUPPLIES

194 yards (176 m) of ¹⁄₁₀-inch (3-mm) macramé cord

Scissors

Wooden rod or tree branch

Fabric dye

Rubber or latex gloves

Hammer and nail, or other hook, as appropriate

1 Cut the cord into sixty-four 3-yard (2.75-m) pieces.

2 Fold a strand of cord in half, wrap the loop around the rod, and pull both strands through the loop to make a larkshead knot. (PHOTO A) Repeat with all sixty-four pieces of cord until the rod is covered with larkshead knots, leaving about 2 inches (5 cm) on each end of the rod knot free.

3 Once all of your larkshead knots are completed, separate a section of eight knots (sixteen cords) to begin making your double half-hitch knots. These eight knots are shown in the photos.

4 To make a double half-hitch knot: Using the strand of yarn that is farthest to the left (this will be the holding cord), place the holding cord over (from left to right) the cord next to it (this will be the working cord), and then under the working cord, then back over itself to form a loop. Pull the knot tightly, and then push it up to the top.

5 Repeat this process again, doing two half-hitch knots to make it a double half-hitch.

6 Working from left to right, complete one row of double half-hitch knots. Once the first row is completed, tie a second row of double half-hitch knots underneath the row you just made, working left to right, pulling the knots tight to push them against your first row.

7 Begin working on your second section of eight knots, using sixteen cords. Begin tying knots from right to left. This will make the knots slope downward toward the first section of knots. Once you have finished your first row of knots, repeat the process to make another row of knots next to the first right to left row. You have now used sixteen of the original larkshead knots. You will, in total, have four of these groupings.

8 Repeat the process of tying two rows of double half-hitch knots, in sections of eight knots, using sixteen cords, working on eight from left to right and then eight from right to left, until you have reached the end of the rod.

CONTINUED ➡

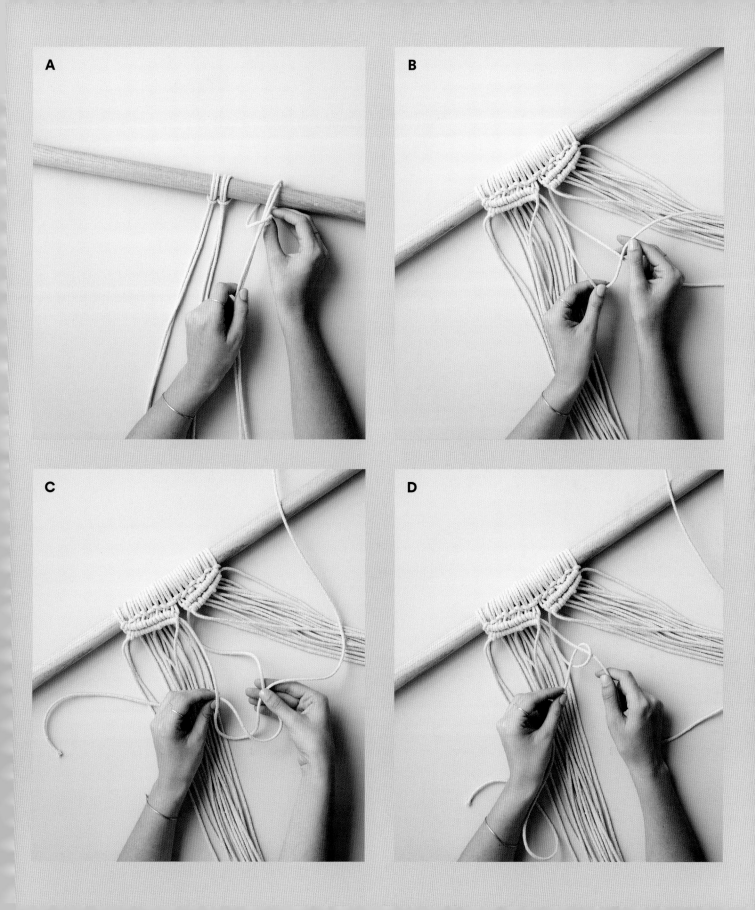

9   Combine the knot sections in their centers by tying two double half-hitch knots at the point where two groups of eight knots meet, pulling tightly. (PHOTOS B, C, D)

10 Once the sections are combined, begin the next row of double half-hitch knots, working in the opposite direction of the knots in the section above. For example, if in the first section of eight knots you worked from left to right, on the section below, you will work from right to left. This will help to create an X pattern where all the sections meet.

11 Continue the process of working in sections of eight, making two rows of double half-hitch knots, alternating from left to right then right to left, and connecting each section of eight with two double half-hitch knots once the section is completed, until you have completed your desired number of tied sections. (We did four rows of knots.) (PHOTO E)

12 Prepare a dye bath according to package directions. We recommend doing this in a bucket that you don't mind discoloring, or in a stainless steel sink. We do not recommend dyeing in a porcelain or fiber glass sink.

13 Put on the gloves and carefully dip an equal portion of the ends of the cords into the bath and soak them according to package directions, or until the desired shade is achieved.

14 Remove the cords from the dye bath and rinse over a bucket or in a stainless steel sink.

15 Hang the wall hanging to dry.

16 Once the wall hanging is dry, cut the cord ends to the desired length. Attach an extra piece of cord to each end of the rod with a knot and hang on a hook or a nail on the wall.

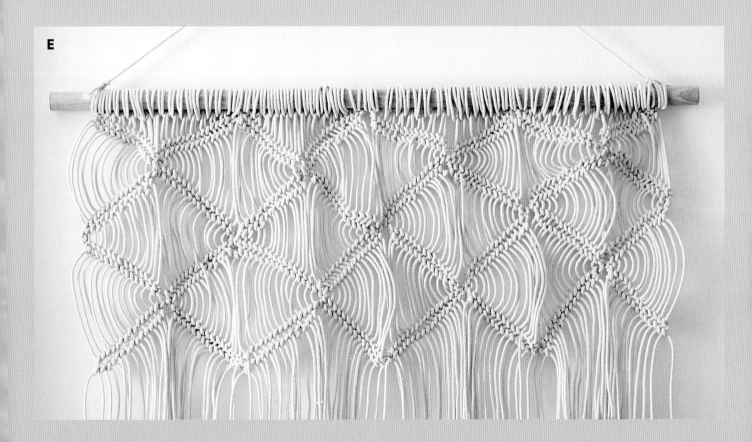
E

MACRAMÉ
LIGHT FIXTURE

Light fixtures can be great statement pieces in your home, and as we saw on the show, they can come in an astounding array of shapes and sizes. One Maker had us swooning over her boho-chic light fixture made from natural hemp that we had to try for ourselves. This stunning macramé version is a similar design and only uses two simple macramé knots so anyone can macra-make it!

SUPPLIES

12-inch (30.5 cm) embroidery hoop

60 yards (55 m) cotton rope, plus 2 yards (1.8 m) for hanging

Scissors

Iron

Wooden craft beads

Light kit (optional)

Drill with ³⁄₁₆-inch (5-mm) bit

2 feet (60 cm) of jewelry chain, cut into four 6-inch (15-cm) pieces

Pliers

4 (¹⁄₁₀-inch/10-mm) jump rings

1. Remove the inner hoop from the embroidery hoop.

2. Cut the rope into approximately 3½-yard (3.2-m) pieces.

3. Once the pieces are cut, unravel the rope into three strands. (PHOTO A)

4. Press the unraveled rope with a hot iron to straighten the strands.

5. Fold a strand of rope in half, wrap the loop around the embroidery hoop, and pull both strands through the loop to secure the rope around the hoop. This is called a larkshead knot. Repeat until the embroidery hoop is fully covered with rope.

6. Working with four strands at a time, tie two outer strands around the inner strands to create a half knot. (PHOTO B) Continue tying half knots, working with four strands at a time, until all the strands have been tied.

7. After completing the first row of half knots, begin the second row of half knots (PHOTO C), using alternating strands from the previous row.

8. Repeat the process until you have four to six rows of half knots in all.

9. Once the rows of half knots are completed, begin making twisting half knots on a group of four strands. The process for making these is no different than for the half knots you have already made, but you will do one half knot after another on the same four strands, and as you tie the strands together they will begin to twist on their own. Repeat these knots twelve to fifteen times, or until you have reached the desired length for your twists. (PHOTO D)

10. Continuing to work in sections of four strands, creating twelve to fifteen twisting half knots all the way around your embroidery hoop.

11. Once all of your twists are complete, repeat steps 6–8, making half knot rows along the base of your twists, using pairs of strands from adjacent twists, to finish your knots. (PHOTO E) Repeat to make four to six rows of knots in all. (PHOTO F)

CONTINUED ➡

A

B

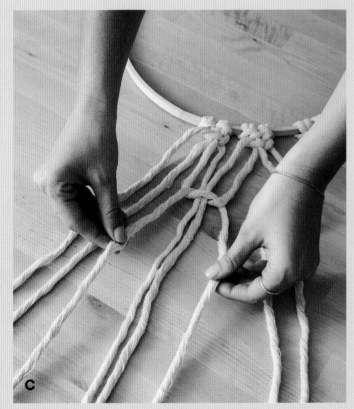

C

D

E

F

12 To attach beads, cut a 10-inch (25-cm) piece of rope. Thread the rope through the light fixture and through an interior piece of rope, approximately 2 inches (5 cm) from the top of the light fixture. Tie off to an interior piece of rope that is not visible from outside the light fixture with a knot to secure. (PHOTO G)

13 String six to eight beads on the loose end of the rope on the exterior of the light fixture.

14 Thread the end of the beaded rope back through the light fixture and through an interior piece of rope, level to where the other end of the rope is tied. Secure with a knot to an interior piece of rope that is not visible from outside the light fixture. (PHOTO H)

15 Repeat this process with sections of rope and beads until a circle of beads loops around the entire light fixture.

G

between the holes in the center of the hoop it would form a plus sign.

19 Using pliers, attach jump rings to each hole in the embroidery hoop.

Attach a 6-inch (5-cm) piece of jewelry chain to each jump ring using pliers.

20 Attach the chains to the light kit and the light fixture.

21 Connect light kit to power source and install according to package directions. If needed, tie a rope to each side of the hoop and hang.

16 Using scissors, trim the ends of your strands at the bottom of the light fixture so they are even.

17 If installing the fixture without a light kit, tie a rope to each side of the hoop and hang it (as shown in finished project photo).

18 If installing a light kit, drill four holes directly across from each other in the embroidery hoop so that if you were to draw a line

TIP: This lovely design would also make a darling baby mobile. Just cut the ends of the rope a bit shorter with scissors, paint the beads in soft pastels, and hang it above your baby's crib for some sweet dreams.

BUCKET SEATS

Ever felt as though you needed more seating in your backyard AND more storage space at the same time? We watched a Maker create these clever seats from 5-gallon buckets that are both functional and stylish—what more could you want? With easily customizable features, like the rope (that you can paint) or the fabric top (that you can embellish), these seats are great for the backyard or even for a kid's room (hello toy storage!).

SUPPLIES

Three 5-gallon (19-L) buckets with lids

⅜-inch (1-cm) twisted sisal rope (about 75 feet/ 23 m) for each bucket)

Hot glue gun filled with glue

Three 24-inch (60-cm) squares of 2-inch-thick (5-cm) high-density foam

Marker

Utility knife

Outdoor tablecloth

Pom-pom trim

Scissors

1. Carefully remove the handle from the bucket by pulling on either side of the bucket and removing the metal part of the handle from its holes. Discard handle.

2. Starting at the base of the bucket, attach the end of the rope to the base of the bucket using a generous amount of hot glue.

3. Begin wrapping the rope around the bucket in a single layer, securing the rope to the bucket with hot glue as you go. Continue wrapping and gluing the rope until the bucket is completely covered with rope. Set aside. (PHOTO A)

4. Place the bucket lid on top of a square of foam and trace with a marker.

5. Cut out the foam along the traced line with a utility knife.

6. Cut out a 16-inch (40.5-cm) square from the tablecloth using scissors.

7. Lay out the tablecloth square, plastic side down, and place the foam circle on top.

8. Fold a corner of the tablecloth over the foam circle and secure the cloth with glue (this side will be the bottom of the bucket cushion). (PHOTO B) Repeat the process of folding the edge of the tablecloth over the foam and glueing, pulling tightly to secure the cloth, until the top and edges of the cushion are completely (and snugly) covered with fabric.

9. Adhere the cushion with the glued side facing down to the top of the bucket lid using a generous amount of hot glue. (PHOTO C)

10. Attach the pom-pom trim around the edge of the bucket lid using hot glue. Use scissors to cut off excess trim. (PHOTO D)

11. Snap the lid onto the bucket seat, pressing tightly to secure the lid.

12. Repeat steps 1–11 to create two more buckets seats.

~~~~~~~~~~~~~~~~~~~~~~~~~~~~

TIP: Use a plastic tablecloth to cover them as shown here and they become waterproof—someone pour us a lemonade!

SUBMARINE
MAILBOX

Special delivery! Making can help you create a beautiful home that reflects who you are, and the first thing that people see when they come over is your mailbox. Clever creations like this yellow submarine mailbox add the ultimate curb appeal to your home. It's truly *sub*-lime.

SUPPLIES

Drill with ³⁄₁₆-inch (5-mm) bit

Plain plastic or metal mailbox in a light color

Spray paint (yellow, red)

Paintbrush

Multi-surface acrylic paint (red, blue, white)

Clear sealant

Nine 2-inch (5-cm) wooden discs

Eight 1½-inch (4-cm) wooden discs

Two 3-inch (7.5-cm) wooden circles

PVC 90-degree-elbow pipe fitting

PVC coupling pipe (just narrow enough to fit inside the elbow piece and add height)

Thin, square sheet of red foam

Scissors

Hot glue gun filled with glue

Wooden kebob skewer

Pencil

1. Using a drill, make a small hole centered in the back of the mailbox.

2. Paint the mailbox yellow using spray paint. Apply several even coats, letting the paint dry completely between each coat. (PHOTO A)

3. Using red spray paint, paint the PVC pipe pieces. Let them dry.

4. Using a paintbrush and acrylic paint, paint 8 of the 2-inch (5-cm) discs red and the 1½-inch (4-cm) discs blue. Additionally, paint one of the 3-inch (7.5-cm) discs blue and the other red. Paint the remaining 2-inch (5-cm) disc blue. Apply two coats on each one and let them dry completely.

5. Make the propeller by creating a pinwheel with the square of foam. First, fold the square, corner to corner, then unfold. These folds will create a template for cutting.

6. Make a pencil mark about 1/3 of the way from center on each of the fold lines.

7. Cut along fold lines, stopping at the pencil mark on each line.

8. Bring every other point of paper into the center and secure with hot glue.

9. Once all the painted pieces are dry, assemble the submarine. Using a hot glue gun, glue the eight 1½-inch (4-cm) blue circles onto the eight 2-inch (5-cm) red circles. Additionally, glue the remaining 2-inch (5-cm) blue circle onto the 3-inch (7.5-cm) red circle. (PHOTO B)

10. Once the red and blue circles are secure, glue the 8 smaller circles to each side of the mailbox (4 on each side) in an even, horizontal line to create portholes. Glue the larger, remaining red and blue circle to the door of the mailbox to create a front porthole.

11. Using a paintbrush and acrylic paint, paint a large white circle on the top of the mailbox. Apply several coats until the circle is even and then let the paint dry completely. Paint a red,

CONTINUED ➡

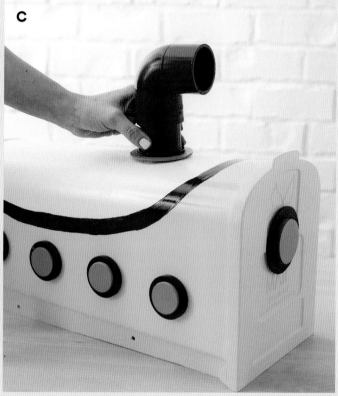

½-inch (1.3-cm) border around the circle. Apply several coats until the border is even and then let the paint dry completely.

12 Glue the 3-inch (7.5-cm) blue disc to the top of the mailbox, a few inches from the door.

13 Slip the coupling pipe into the elbow pipe to create the periscope. Glue the base of the periscope onto the blue disc with the opening of the scope facing toward the mailbox door. (PHOTO C)

14 Feed the wooden skewer through the hole and through the center of the foam pinwheel. (PHOTO D)

15 Secure the skewer to the interior of mailbox and to the pinwheel using hot glue.

16 Using scissors, trim excess length from the wooden skewer inside the mailbox.

17 Spray the mailbox with two coats of clear sealant to seal and protect the paint. Let the sealant dry completely between coats.

18 Mount the mailbox according to directions.

As a DIY designer, I am ever evolving. From being resourceful in making creations using simple materials to designing innovative DIY templates, my focus is on helping others create for their families and their businesses. Being able to share my love for creating was highlighted while I was on *Making It*. On so many levels, my time on the show was an experience of immense growth for me, both personally and professionally. I had to step out of my comfort zone in leaps and bounds. Not only did I conquer my fear of flying (I hadn't been on a plane in more than fifteen years!), but I also had to navigate through being away from my husband and kids while being on the West Coast to film the show. Every day on set, I strived to be the best version of myself. I learned so much from the amazing artists who worked alongside me in the barn. Genuine admiration and respect for each other's unique talents led to new friendships. Although we all live in different parts of the country, we still keep in touch often. We were a crazy bunch, but we formed a strong bond . . . like hot glue!

The project that I most enjoyed designing and making was the Treehouse Mailbox, which was a house made out of foamboard with a mini handmade clay paint roller, glue gun, popcorn buckets, and DVDs to represent my family. The tiny paint roller and glue gun represent my husband, Anthony, and I, as we are always making something. The mailbox is being supported by a balloon tree post, symbolizing the Creative Heart Studio brand that we are building to support our family. The DVDs and popcorn buckets represent something we love doing together as a family. By using a variety of mediums, I was able to create a meaningful, visual sneak peek of my favorite people in my favorite place: my family at home.

Making It gave me the greatest opportunity of my career, where I was able to proudly showcase my passion while teaching my kids to always reach for the stars.

ANIMAL HOUSE

Whether you have a cat or a dog or a bunny or a turtle, a fun and friendly home for your best animal bud is a great way to show off your own style—or theirs! Inspired by a Master Craft challenge to create the ultimate pet home, we recommend this chic pet house, perfect for all the good dogs out there. This dog house is minimalist and only requires a few very basic tools and supplies. Plus, all of the cuts to the wooden dowels and molding can be made in a snap at your local home-improvement store.

SUPPLIES

⅜-inch (1-cm) wood dowels, cut into five 21-inch (53-cm) pieces

Drill with ⅜-inch (1-cm) drill bit

Wood molding, cut into two 26-inch (66-cm) pieces and eight 18-inch (46-cm) pieces

Wood glue

2½ yards (2.3 m) fabric, cut 20 inches (51 cm) wide

Hot glue gun filled with glue

1 Drill ⅜-inch (1-cm) holes into each of the molding pieces, 1 inch (2.5-cm) from each end. (PHOTO A)

2 Assemble each side of the frame first, using two dowels and two pieces of molding to form a square, applying wood glue to the ends of the dowels before inserting them into the molding pieces. Attach the two sides together on the bottom by gluing two molding pieces to the dowel ends, one in the front and one in the back. Now build the top: Using one dowel, attach two molding pieces on either end, splayed out in a V shape. Attach the molding pieces at the V ends to the tops of each side, in the front and the back. You now have a fully formed house shape. Let dry. (PHOTO B, C)

3 Wrap one end of the fabric around one of the dowels that forms the base of the house, and secure the fabric with hot glue. (PHOTO D)

4 Carefully pull the fabric up and over the top of the house, and secure the fabric on the other side with hot glue. Cut off excess fabric if necessary. (PHOTO E, F)

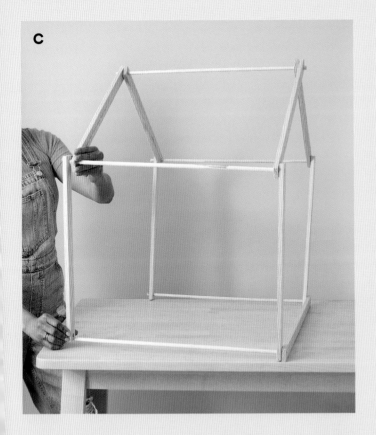

STREAMER
PHOTO BACKDROP

〰〰〰〰〰〰〰〰〰〰〰

Is it really a party if you don't have a bold backdrop to snap pics against? This party streamer backdrop looks like a deconstructed piñata and is sure to be a smash at your next soiree. Stick to a simple color palette or use all the colors of the rainbow; either way, your partygoers won't be able to resist posing. Say cheese!

SUPPLIES

4 by 10-foot (1.2 by 3-m) section of plastic temporary fencing

Scissors

Thumbtacks or nails

5-6 rolls jumbo crepe paper streamer (about 500 feet per roll) in various colors

Glue dot dispenser or hot glue gun filled with glue

1 Cut the fencing to desired back-drop width using scissors (ours was 10 feet wide).

2 Hang the fencing on the wall using tacks or nails (or assemble the backdrop on the floor and then hang once assembled).

3 Cut up the crepe paper streamers into sections of various lengths (i.e., a bunch of 12-inch [30.5-cm] streamers, a bunch of 8-inch [20-cm] streamers, etc.).

4 Starting at the bottom of the fenc-ing, attach the streamers by looping them through the holes in the fencing and securing each streamer with a dot of glue. (PHOTO A)

5 Working horizontally in clusters of each color, continue to densely fill the holes in the fencing with crepe paper streamers, avoiding any gaps, until you've completed one horizontal row. (PHOTO B)

6 Repeat the process, working in clus-ters of each color from left to right, horizontally, moving from the bot-tom to the top until the fencing is densely covered with crepe paper.

A child of the eighties, I grew up loving Ninja Turtles and for a few brief stints actually had turtles as pets. I say "brief" because turtles are escape artists. Inevitably, every single one of my turtles got away. What most people don't know is that turtles are quite crafty. Masters of subterfuge, they do nothing while you watch them. When you finally get bored and leave the room, they start doing calisthenics, tai chi, and turtle-jitsu and working on their hops. I don't blame them—freedom is a powerful impulse, and no one wants to live in a fish tank. A home, after all, should reflect your personality and cultural tastes!

Creating this little narrative as the inspiration for my project for the Animal House challenge allowed me to get playful with the details. I imagined that my turtle was a martial arts enthusiast, so why not make the house look like a samurai helmet? The face mask was made from plywood and detailed using paint and a rotary tool. It functioned as the arched opening to the turtle house while simultaneously discouraging any unwanted visitors. Turtles love their peace and quiet, after all. Leading into the interior is a felt throw rug that is shaped like a tongue. There are two teacups inside the house—the left one

holds water, and the right one contains a nice tasty salad of moss. Continuing that notion of easy access to food, I used moss patches as the siding for the outer panels of the helmet. Given the choice, who wouldn't want edible walls? To keep it fun, I also peppered other turtle shell details throughout the piece.

My advice for makers is to always look for ways to incorporate interesting quirks and humorous nuances into your project. Don't be afraid to make things a little funky; that's the beauty of things that are handmade—they are uniquely you!

BALLOON ARCH

One of the best parts about being a Maker is taking something that's been around forever and finding a way to make it fresh and new. Balloons have always been a party staple, but in the last couple of years, Makers have been creating colorful, cascading balloon installations that can help bring new life to the most basic of parties. Executing your own bubbly balloon arch is easier than you'd think, so pull out your pump and let's party!

SUPPLIES

Three to five 36-inch (90-cm) balloons in various colors

Forty to fifty 12-inch (30-cm) balloons in various colors

Twenty to thirty 6-inch (15-cm) balloons in various colors

Balloon pump

Removable wall hooks

Floral wire

Masking tape

Fifteen to twenty paper fans and lanterns

Glue dot dispenser or hot glue gun filled with glue

1 Blow up the balloons using a balloon pump.

2 Attach hooks around the window or doorway where you will be hanging the completed arch, using approximately one hook per 2 feet (60-cm) of arch.

3 Tie the balloon necks together in clusters of four balloons (excluding the 36-inch/90-cm balloons). (PHOTO A)

4 Join the balloon clusters together by wrapping floral wire around the tied necks of one cluster and then the tied necks of another cluster. (To prevent the wire from popping the balloons, fold down the ends and wrap them with masking tape.) (PHOTO B)

5 Work in the 36-inch (90-cm) balloons every few feet, attaching them with wire the same way you attached the smaller clusters to each other. When you are finished, you will have a chain that incorporates all the balloons.

6 To form the arch, hang the wired clusters on the wall hooks, using hot glue or a glue dot to secure the clusters, if desired. (PHOTO C)

7 Once the entire balloon arch is hung on the hooks, fill in any gaps with paper lanterns and fans, securing them with glue dots where needed.

A

B

C

TIP: Looking to have a more formal or earthy vibe for your soiree? Add in some greenery or flowers among the balloons! A touch of plants is sure to make your arch even more pleasing.

GLOSSARY

BEESWAX: Beeswax can be used as a polish on furniture to seal and protect wood. It is a natural option for enhancing shine.

BLANKET STITCH: A basic embroidery stitch that is often used along the edge of a fabric hem, or to stitch elements in place in an embroidery project. It is created by making open half-loops of stitching, one after another.

COTTON BATTING: Light, soft, cotton fibers formed into layers, often used for filling quilts, pillows, stuffed animals, etc.

EPOXY RESIN: A glossy, clear polymer that can be used to coat all kinds of surfaces to give them a clear finish. Epoxy resin comes in two parts: a resin and a hardener. Mixing the resin and hardener together prompts a chemical reaction, transforming them from a liquid into a solid.

EYELET: A small ring of metal that is used to reinforce a hole in a piece of fabric. There are generally two parts to an eyelet (either a top ring and a bottom ring, or a single ring that can be folded in half with an eyelet setter), and when pressure is applied with an eyelet setter, they create an enclosed hole in fabric or paper.

EYELET SETTER: An eyelet setter connects the top and bottom ring of an eyelet to create a protected metal circle, generally around a hole in fabric or paper. They come as tools that act and look like a hole punch, tools that are spring-loaded, or tools that are simply a metal post that is hit with a hammer to connect the eyelets.

FABRIC MEDIUM: A paint-like product that can be mixed with paint to achieve a softer, more flexible paint when painting on fabric.

FLORAL FOAM: A specialized foam used to stabilize flowers in an arrangement. Floral foam is softer and slightly more malleable than craft foam and can hold water to increase longevity in fresh flower arrangements.

FLORAL WIRE: Floral wire is flexible aluminum wire generally used in floral design. It is often coated with a thin layer of colored paint (usually a shade of green) to help it blend in with foliage, but can also be found in silver or white. Floral wire is measured in thickness, or gauge.

FOAM TAPE: A durable, double-sided tape with a layer of foam in the center, ideal for bonding, attaching, and mounting.

JEWELRY CHAIN: Loose chain, often sold in spools, that is typically used to make jewelry. Jewelry chain comes in a wide array of weights, finishes, and lengths.

JIGSAW: Jigsaws are primarily used to make curved, intricate cuts in wood but can also be used to make plunge cuts, straight cuts, and bevel cuts. Along with wood, jigsaws can cut through materials like plastic, sheet metals, and ceramic tile.

LACQUER: A range of clear or colored wood finishes that dry by solvent evaporation or a curing process that produces a hard, durable finish.

LIGHT KIT: A light kit (or swag kit) is a plug-in lighting solution that includes the materials needed to install a light fixture by plugging it into the wall instead of to the interior electric wiring of a space.

LINSEED OIL: Also known as flaxseed oil or flax oil, linseed oil is a colorless to yellowish oil obtained from the dried, ripened seeds of the flax plant. It is used as a preservative for wood, leaving a shiny but not glossy surface that shows the grain of the wood.

MACRAMÉ: Macramé is a form of textile or fiber art produced by using knotting techniques. Materials used in macramé include cords made of cotton twine, linen, hemp, jute, leather, or yarn. Macramé can be used to make everything from wall hangings and plant hangers to jewelry, purses, and even clothing.

MITER SAW: A specialized saw that allows users to cut at a variety of angles.

PASTE WAX: A thick, creamy wax that, when buffed into wood, can add a vibrant shine and glossy finish.

PEGBOARD: A board with a regular pattern of small holes. Pegboards are generally used to hang and organize as the holes accept pegs or hooks.

POLY-FIL (OR POLYESTER FIBERFILL): A synthetic fiber used for stuffing pillows and other soft objects, such as stuffed animals.

POLYURETHANE: A paint or varnish finish, generally applied with a paintbrush, that dries clear and provides a protective seal for wood.

PRINTABLE HEAT TRANSFER VINYL: A craft vinyl that can be customized with graphics or designs using a printer. Once a design is printed on the vinyl, it can then be applied permanently to fabric using an iron.

PVC COUPLING PIPE: Couplings are one of the most simple types of PVC fittings. They are a small part that connects or "couples" one part to another, found in the plumbing aisle at home improvement stores.

ROVING: Roving is a thick, bulky yarn that is not twisted or plied like many types of yarn and is often used to give a rustic look to projects.

SHELLAC: Shellac is a warm-colored finish for wood that is applied with a rag, brush, or sprayer. It produces a very fine, mellow finish and accentuates the natural grain of the wood.

SILK SCREENING: A printing/stenciling technique for fabric that involves printing ink through stencils that are supported by a porous fabric mesh stretched across a frame called a screen.

SPRAY SEALANT: A clear sealer found in the spray paint aisle that protects and seals painted surfaces.

SYNTHETIC DYE: A dye specially made for synthetic fabrics like polyester, polyester cotton blends, acrylic, and acetate.

TEMPORARY FENCING: Plastic fencing generally found in a roll at a home improvement store, used to create a temporary barrier for construction sites or other events.

TURNING TOOL: A cylindrical tool used in sewing to reach inside a narrow tube of fabric and turn it right side out.

VARNISH: A clear, hard, protective finish or film. Varnish is applied over wood stains as a final step to achieve a film for gloss and protection.

YARN NEEDLE: Yarn needles are larger needles, commonly made of plastic. They are available in different sizes to fit the various weights of yarn. The tip of a yarn needle is less sharp than a sewing needle, and the eye is larger for greater ease when threading.

TEMPLATES AND DIAGRAMS

CROSS-STITCH WALL ART

page 143

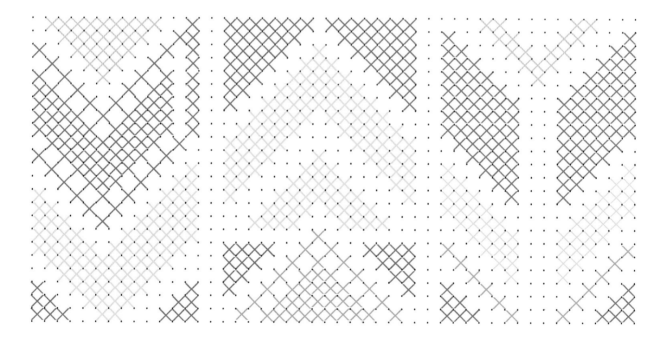

ANIMAL INSTINCTS

page 121, shown at 20%

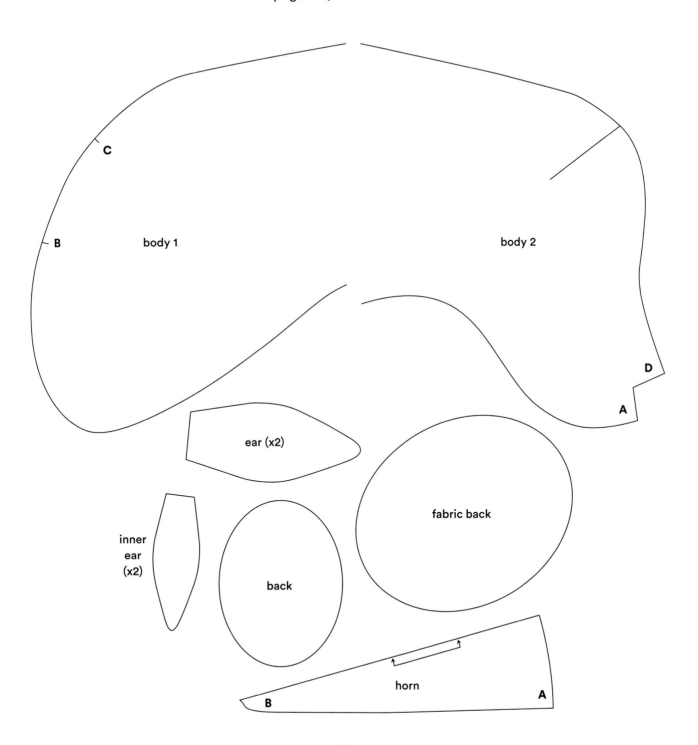

PAPER FLORAL CENTERPIECE AND UNCONVENTIONAL DOOR WREATH

pages 67 and 115, shown at 40%

FLOWER 1

FLOWER 2

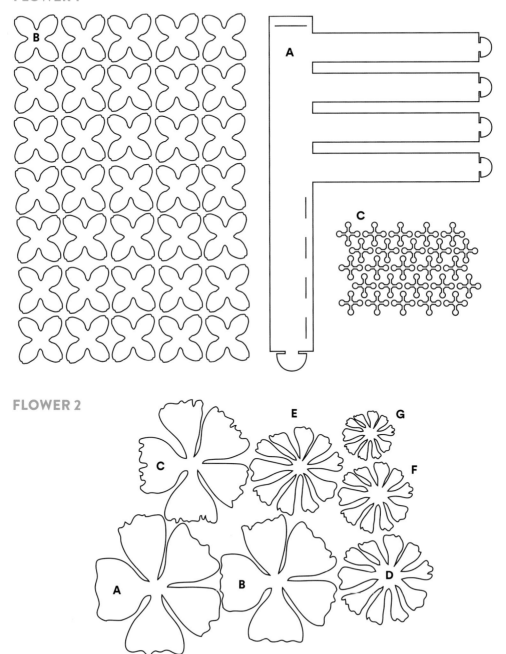

FLOWER 3

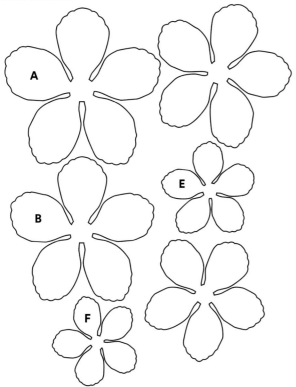

FLOWER 4

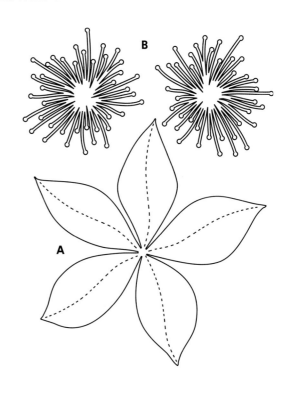

FLOWER 5

FLOWER 5

YOU ARE WHAT YOU EAT

page 99, shown at 30%

FELT TACO

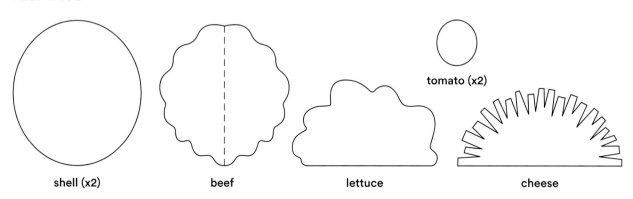

shell (x2)   beef   lettuce   tomato (x2)   cheese

FELT PIZZA

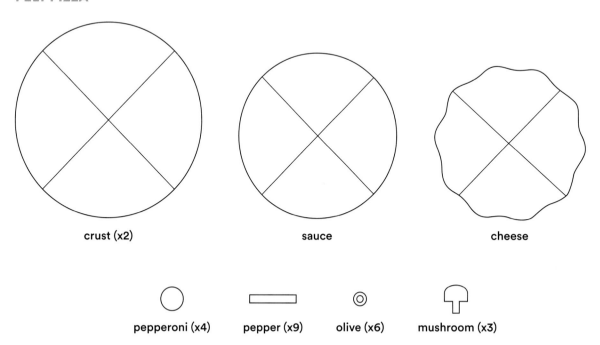

crust (x2)   sauce   cheese

pepperoni (x4)   pepper (x9)   olive (x6)   mushroom (x3)

FELT CHEESEBURGER

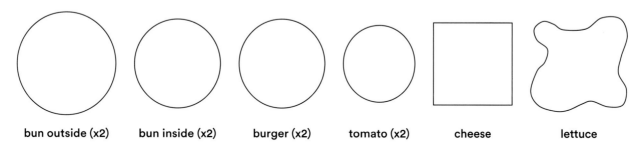

bun outside (x2)   bun inside (x2)   burger (x2)   tomato (x2)   cheese   lettuce

FELT ICE CREAM

FELT ICE POPS

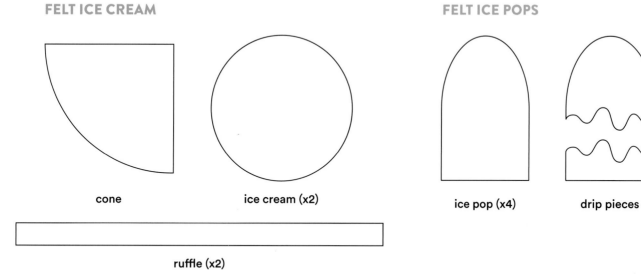

cone   ice cream (x2)

ice pop (x4)   drip pieces

ruffle (x2)

FOOD TRUCK

page 137

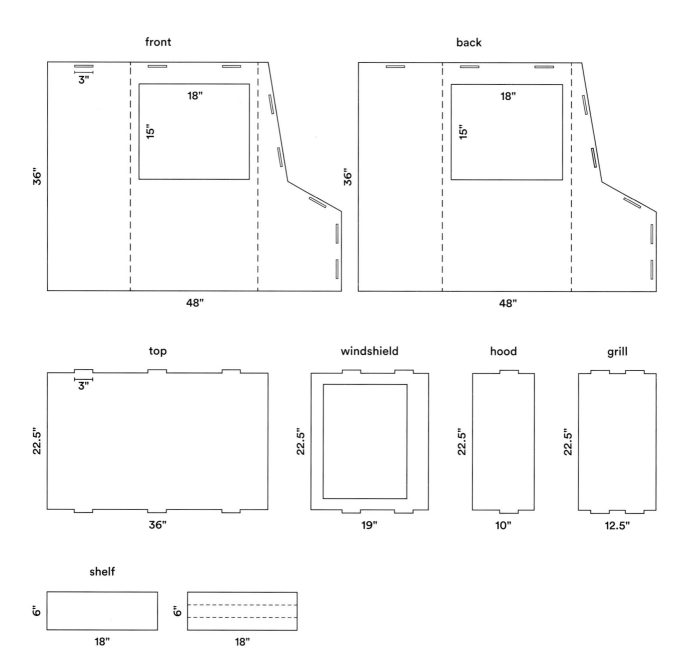

front

3"

18"

15"

36"

48"

back

18"

15"

36"

48"

top

3"

22.5"

36"

windshield

22.5"

19"

hood

22.5"

10"

grill

22.5"

12.5"

shelf

6"

18"

6"

18"

ACKNOWLEDGMENTS

Many thanks to Nick Offerman, Dayna Isom Johnson, and James DiResta, for the words of wisdom and encouragement that they shared.

A special thank-you to the Makers, for their contributions and project inspiration.

Jo Gick: follow her @ohsojo_ and at joannagick.com.
Jamie Hudson: follow him @20Leagues and at 20Leagues.com.
Amber Kemp-Gerstel: follow her @DamaskLove and at damasklove.com.
Billy Kheel: follow him @bkheel and at bkheel.com.
Rebecca Propes: follow her @rebeccaDIY and at rebeccapropes.com.
Justine Silva: follow her @justine.silva.
Matt Ortiz
Lilly Jimenez: follow her @thecreativeheartstudio and at thecreativeheartstudio.com.

Thank you to all the cast and crew of the show and to all who participated in making this book come to life, especially:

Nick Offerman	Jenny Groom	Neysa Siefert
Amy Poehler	Vince Klaseus	Kathleen Smyth
Meredith Ahr	Gerry Logue	Lee Straus
Aaron Bastian	Rebecca Marks	Chip Sullivan
Joni Camacho	Brad Melnick	Paul Telegdy
George Cheeks	Daniel Posener	Nicolle Yaron
Emmanuel Doessant	Traci Saulsberry	Eowyn Mishawn
Corey Fitelson	George Sealy	Neil Casey
Len Fogge	Shelby Shaftel	Whitney Welch

We would like to thank the following for their generous donations of materials that enabled this book to be all that it could be:

ArtMinds	The Felt Store	Plaid Crafts
Astrobrights	Fiskars	Silhouette America
ColorShot	Jamie Lane Designs	We Are Knitters
Darice	Nic Squirrel	

This book was made by many hands, and it was incredible to combine so many geniuses into a dream team.

Thank you to my true partner in the making of this book, my sister/therapist/creative advisor/ cheerleader, Sam. Your endless hours of work, support, and creative vision made this whole thing not only happen, but really sparkle. Thank you, forever!

To Shawna at Abrams, for taking such a big chance on me and for giving me my dream job. I am so grateful for your generosity toward me. To Meredith, your wisdom, hustle, and gifts shaped this book (and this experience) from something that felt impossible into something full of color and happiness and inspiration. You are a total boss and are just the best.

To Nicole Hill Gerulat, a true force of nature, for her unreal talents shooting this book and for her exceptional taste in nineties hip-hop. To Veronica Olson and Taylor Olson, for their incredible styling genius. I will forever find myself asking "What would Veronica do?" whenever I am trying to make something more beautiful.

Biggest thank-you to all the people who didn't hesitate for a second when I begged them to have mercy on me and share their skills. To Caroline Lefebvre, for her gorgeous unicorn pattern. To Andy Curtis, for his day-saving carpentry skills, and Elise Curtis, for being an essential member of my and Sam's team. To Caitlin Probst and Raylan Probst, for making the dog house shot perfect. To Kara Hurst, for so generously sharing her sewing skills. To Kristin, for her child-whispering powers. To Alex, for his patience in the chaos. Thank you to all the family cheerleaders (Megan Morgan, Dev, Jer, Erica, Meg, the Welkers) and to Mom and Dad. So full of gratitude for each of you. To Redder and Willa, for their modeling talents and snuggles. And to Adam, who can always make me laugh (even in the midst of a macramé crisis) and who believed in me every second. "Making It" only matters if I'm with you.

—Liz Welker, cofounder of The Pretty Life Girls, follow her @prettylifegirls

Editor: Meredith A. Clark
Designer: Danielle Youngsmith
Production Manager: Alison Gervais

Library of Congress Control Number: 2019944013

ISBN: 978-1-4197-4348-1
eISBN: 978-1-68335-882-4

Copyright © 2020 Universal Television LLC
Making It copyright © 2020 Universal Television LLC. All rights reserved.

Foreword copyright © 2020 Nick Offerman

Text written by Liz Welker
Photography by Nicole Hill Gerulat
Images on page 8 copyright © 2020 Patrick Roberts

Introduction by Dayna Isom Johnson

Published in 2020 by Abrams, an imprint of ABRAMS. All rights reserved.
No portion of this book may be reproduced, stored in a retrieval system,
or transmitted in any form or by any means, mechanical, electronic,
photocopying, recording, or otherwise, without written permission from
the publisher.

Printed and bound in China
10 9 8 7 6 5 4 3 2 1

Abrams books are available at special discounts when purchased in quantity
for premiums and promotions as well as fundraising or educational use.
Special editions can also be created to specification. For details, contact
specialsales@abramsbooks.com or the address below.

Abrams® is a registered trademark of Harry N. Abrams, Inc.

ABRAMS The Art of Books
195 Broadway, New York, NY 10007
abramsbooks.com